PRAISE FOR *VERTICAL MARRIAGE*

Vertical Marriage is a weighty (I mean that in the best sense of the word), no-holds-barred approach to get your marriage started on the right spiritual footing. Wise and spiritually penetrating, this book is an ideal way to spiritually test your relationship and understand its biblical foundation. As an added treat, it also offers much practical, real-world advice to help you on the journey toward marital intimacy in all aspects. Highly recommended, especially for serious believers.

—GARY THOMAS
AUTHOR, *SACRED MARRIAGE* AND *THE SACRED SEARCH*

There is a great difference between a marriage that "gets by" — and one that is lived in light of eternity. Mike and Anne Rizzo lift our vision here, with *Vertical Marriage*. Their own marriage is a testimony, and this book offers the reader a powerful blueprint for a beautiful union that will help any couple, young or old, to revive their perspective on deep partnership and worship.

—SARA HAGERTY
AUTHOR, *EVERY BITTER THING IS SWEET*

It is an honor to recommend this amazing resource! In a time of great confusion and unnecessary complexities this book draws a distinct arrow to the heart of Jesus and truth of the Bible! We ought to believe day and night for a restoration of families to their intended design . . . and yet know it starts with each one of us!

—ANDY BYRD
CO-FOUNDER, FIRE AND FRAGRANCE MINISTRIES
CO-FOUNDER, CIRCUIT RIDERS
YWAM KONA

I believe that one of the wisest things an engaged couple can do is give themselves to a time of preparation before their wedding day. This manual contains not only the practical points of preparation, but will also challenge you to lay the spiritual bedrock foundation of your marriage before you say "I do."

—JUSTIN RIZZO
Worship Leader and Songwriter

Wisdom has been defined as the ability to live life skillfully. In this book, Mike and Anne have crafted a tremendous tool to help you navigate your courtship skillfully. Their wisdom will prepare you for a loving marriage filled with joy and hope — with Jesus at the center. I recommend this one highly!

—BOB SORGE
Author, bobsorge.com

I am captivated by eternity and fixated on living a life that will bear eternal fruit, so I've reached to live before the One who will evaluate my life in the end. As Mike and Anne Rizzo share in *Vertical Marriage*, "The hour in which we live is not a time to cast off restraint or focus on the temporal; it's a time for husbands and wives to contend for fresh, eternal vision in their marriages." If you are considering marriage, never let go of the highest vision — living for the audience of One. This book will give you tools to love Him and to grow in love for one another.

— MISTY EDWARDS
Worship Leader and Songwriter

Testimonials

I like riding motorcycles and shooting guns, so I was apprehensive about meeting with some people to talk about feelings and emotional expectations. My guard was quickly lowered as I realized that the Rizzos were full of practical wisdom and didn't overwhelm me with poems and perfume. They had a very realistic approach to romance and sexuality that didn't take anything away from the excitement of being in love, but also helped us maintain "real life" expectations. It has been almost exactly a year since my wife and I sat with Mike and Anne, and we can clearly look back on specific times that we have purposefully put their teachings into practice. I truly believe that our sessions have helped to enrich our marriage!

—Jim & Natalie

It is foolish to get married without first doing premarital counseling. It would also be foolish to not get the manual currently in your hand. Mike and Anne have a great wealth of wisdom and knowledge when it comes to relationships, and they helped my wife and I realize the deep significance of the commitment we were making to each other when we got married. We absolutely love them, and you will too.

—Eric & Erin

Through this book, Mike and Anne are joining your team in your fight for love. My husband and I have found the Rizzos' experience and knowledge completely priceless, and I can't recommend them highly enough!

—Lauren & Mitch

Mike and Anne are seasoned counselors and friends of the Lord. Premarital counseling was a joy with them, even as we walked through some tough places of the heart. They painted a much-needed, biblical perspective on marriage in light of eternity and our callings to love God first.

—Ailene & Carl

My wife and I were so glad we did premarital counseling with the Rizzos. Our time with them pinpointed areas of weakness and gave us some tools to grow: like resolving conflict and defining the roles in our relationship. Because of these conversations, we went into marriage empowered to move forward as a team.

—BRIAN & JOANNIE

Mike and Anne Rizzo were a well of deep wisdom to drink from as we made huge decisions that greatly impacted our future. They were able to read deeply into our hearts and tell us things that we were thinking and feeling but couldn't really articulate. Their advice has stuck with us, making our marriage stable and strong, and is still shaping the way we live day by day, three years later.

—NATE & KATE

AN INTERNATIONAL HOUSE OF PRAYER AUTHOR

VERTICAL MARRIAGE

A Godward Preparation for Life Together

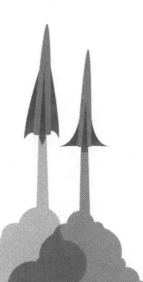

MIKE & ANNE RIZZO

FOREWORD BY MIKE & DIANE BICKLE

FORERUNNER PUBLISHING
KANSAS CITY, MISSOURI

Vertical Marriage — A Godward Preparation for Life Together by Mike and Anne Rizzo

Published by Forerunner Publishing
International House of Prayer
3535 E. Red Bridge Road
Kansas City, Missouri 64137
ihopkc.org/books

ISBN: 978-1-938060-33-5
eBook ISBN: 978-1-938060-34-2

Unless otherwise noted, all Scripture taken from the New King James Version®. Copyright © 1982 by Thomas Nelson. Used by permission. All rights reserved.

Scripture quotations marked (ESV) are from The Holy Bible, English Standard Version® (ESV®), copyright © 2001 by Crossway, a publishing ministry of Good News Publishers. Used by permission. All rights reserved.

Scripture quotations marked (The Message) from THE MESSAGE. Copyright © by Eugene H. Peterson 1993, 1994, 1995, 1996, 2000, 2001, 2002. Used by permission of Tyndale House Publishers, Inc.

Scripture quotations marked (NIV) are taken from the Holy Bible, New International Version®, NIV®. Copyright © 1973, 1978, 1984, 2011 by Biblica, Inc.™ Used by permission of Zondervan. All rights reserved worldwide. www.zondervan.com The "NIV" and "New International Version" are trademarks registered in the United States Patent and Trademark Office by Biblica, Inc.™

Scripture quotations marked PHILLIPS are taken from "The New Testament in Modern English", J. B. Phillips, 1962 edition, published by HarperCollins.

Scripture quotations marked (AMP) taken from the Amplified® Bible, Copyright © 1954, 1958, 1962, 1964, 1965, 1987 by The Lockman Foundation. Used by permission. (www.Lockman.org)

Scripture quotations marked (NASB) taken from the New American Standard Bible®, Copyright © 1960, 1962, 1963, 1968, 1971, 1972, 1973, 1975, 1977, 1995 by The Lockman Foundation. Used by permission. (www.Lockman.org)

Scripture quotations marked (KJV) taken from the King James Bible. Public domain.

All emphasis in Scripture quotations is the author's.

Cover design by Wesley Harmon
Interior design by Lala England
Printed in the United States of America

To Mike Bickle.
Through your teaching and example as a leader,
our lives have been enlarged.

CONTENTS

Acknowledgments xi

Foreword.. xiii

Introduction: Are We Ready for Marriage?............................... 1

Purity Pledge 5

Part One:
Building a Strong Foundation

1: Covenant or Contract.. 13

2: Let's Build a Marriage 25

3: Evaluating the Relationship 33

Part Two:
A Unique Partnership

4: Marital Vision.. 41

5: God's Amazing Design.. 53

6: Husband and Wife Roles and Needs 65

Part Three:
Conflict, Cash, and Sex

7: Resolving Conflict... 77

8: The Healing Journey.. 85

9: Loving God with Our Money 95

10: Sexuality in Marriage 105

Part Four:
Fruit That Remains

11: Marriage Within the Bridal Paradigm 119

12: A Fruitful Investment 125

13: Married in Exile 129

Part Five:
Resources

Appendix A: Birth Control 139

Appendix B: Couples Connecting 145

Appendix C: Household Budget 149

Appendix D: Intercultural Marriage 153

Appendix E: Wedding Night and Honeymoon 155

Appendix F: Divorce and Remarriage 157

Appendix G: Recommended Reading 161

ACKNOWLEDGMENTS

Amy Peterson — your professional skills and excellent coaching have made us better writers. We greatly appreciate your partnership and invaluable contributions to this project.

John Chisholm — without you, this book would not be in existence! Thanks for encouraging us to put a part of our life's work on paper.

Our family — Danielle, Jonathan, Justin, Naomi, and Liberty. We are blessed to be doing life and ministry in your company!

FOREWORD

If you are browsing this book, chances are that you are in a dating or engaged relationship, or you want to be prepared ahead of time for when that happens. The purpose of entering into a dating relationship is to discover if the other person is someone you would want to marry — to get acquainted with their life vision, values, personality, gifts, and weaknesses to decide if you want the relationship to progress to engagement. This manual that Mike and Anne Rizzo have written will help you in this process.

One purpose of engagement is to establish the relational and lifestyle patterns that will be foundational to your marriage relationship. These involve how you will communicate, spend time and money, and solve conflicts, and how you view sexuality, children, raising children, planning the future, seeking God, doing ministry, and relating to the local church. All of these topics, and more, are covered in these pages.

We have found that the best preparation for dating and marriage is to work on yourself. Work through your own brokenness with the help of wise counsel. Grow in your true identity and gain tools to help you continue to live authentically by owning your sin, asking for and extending forgiveness, and taking your thought life captive.

Deep love is built on respect. The most important question is not, "Will I be attracted to this man or woman for the rest of my life?" Attractions can change very quickly. The question is, "Will I respect him or her for the rest of my life?" Are they interesting in ways that go beyond physical attraction? Is his or her heart set on the right things, and do they consistently follow through on their convictions over time?

A strong foundation for godly marriage involves being equally yoked. Each one sets their heart to seek first Jesus and His kingdom, to verbally encourage each other to press in to their relationship with Jesus wholeheartedly, and to obey God's will in their life and relationships.

We love each other more now, at the thirty-eight-year mark of our marriage, than ever before. We believe in humility, serving one another, and obeying Jesus. One purpose of marriage is to develop a strong partnership in doing God's will together as a couple and family. This involves enjoying His blessings, enduring hardships, and obeying Him in small things and the routines of everyday life.

We are so grateful for Mike and Anne's life and ministry at the International House of Prayer — many lives have been changed by it.

Mike & Diane Bickle
International House of Prayer

INTRODUCTION

Are We Ready for Marriage?

Mike

This is a question asked by many singles as they ponder marriage. It is also a question asked by many who are married, feeling overwhelmed by the challenge, and wondering if they made the right decision.

A decision of great magnitude requires great consideration. Jesus made this clear to the multitudes that followed Him: *"If anyone comes to Me and does not hate his father and mother, wife and children, brothers and sisters, yes, and his own life also, he cannot be My disciple"* (Lk. 14:26). This is the essence of being joined to Christ. He must become the transcendent object of love among all of our relationships.

His instruction is to "count the cost" before deciding. The two parables of Jesus' following this passage serve as an illustration (Lk. 14:28–33). One: before you build a tower be sure you have access to all the materials you will need to complete it. Two: before going to war consider your military resources, measured against those of your enemy.

Are we ready to count the cost of what it takes to build a marriage over decades? Are we ready to consider whether we have the strength to stand against the army of darkness that will come against our marriage union? Are we aware that the strength will come only when our relationship with Christ is prioritized above all?

A covenant pledge to Christ is not to be entered into lightly. In like manner, choosing to spend the rest of our earthly days in a marriage covenant with one person requires a skillful and wise decision-making process.

Most of us are familiar with the invitation to receive Christ, given at evangelistic crusades. Various estimates I have seen over the years indicate that a low percent of respondents (anywhere from 6 to 25 percent) continue on in a vibrant faith. Listen to these words of a famous evangelist who preached the gospel in the American colonies during the Great Awakening: "There are so many stony-ground hearers that receive the word with joy, that I have determined to suspend my judgment, till I know the tree by its fruits."[1] The evangelist was George Whitefield.

I advise singles who think they have found their marriage partner to first evaluate their ability to build a solid foundation in the relationship, which rests on the reality of each partner's commitment to Jesus. Only marriages with a vertical focus on God successfully enter into all that He designed marriage to be. The sets of questions throughout this manual are for self-examination as well as a lens through which to evaluate that potential future spouse. Is the fruit of the Spirit evident? How have we navigated seasons of transition? Have we walked with Christ, rooted and built up in Him, established in the faith (see Colossians 2:7)?

In our own premarital season, Anne asked these same questions of me and I of her. As our friendship was initially budding with promise of perhaps a longer future, we began to count the cost and take stock of our relational resources. Throughout this book we have both endeavored to share highlights of our journey with you, and you will note our names prior to each major section.

My life in Christ is the ultimate source for my married life. Granted, I don't always feel qualified, much less prepared, to run hard after God every day. Nor do I rely on feeling like a great husband to determine whether I choose to act like one. But *if we count the cost on the front end of every day and nurture the "Yes, Lord" on the inside, His grace will be sufficient. Together, your source in God will be the source in your marriage.*

Nearing thirty-five years of marriage at this writing, I am filled with contented reflection, looking back over decades of partnership with my wife. *"For I am already being poured out as a drink offering, and the time of my departure is at hand. I have fought the good fight, I have finished the race, I have kept the faith"* (2 Tim. 4:6–7). Seeking to pour out my life daily is what will enable me in the end to look back on a life poured out. *Husbands and wives who find common ground here, will go the distance.*

From another perspective, Jesus described it as laying up *"treasures in heaven, where neither moth nor rust destroys and where thieves do not break in and steal"* (Mt. 6:20). Divided allegiance, the attempt to serve two masters, results in both treasure and heart remaining earthbound and exposed to loss. A husband and wife who join forces unto this end make a powerful team!

Consider Second Corinthians 4:11–12: *"For we who live are always being given over to death for Jesus' sake, so that the life of Jesus also may be manifested in our mortal flesh. So death is at work in us, but life in you"* (ESV). Every believer has read this passage at one time or another and felt a connection to the hardships Paul lists in preceding verses: afflicted, hedged in, perplexed, persecuted, struck down. The key phrase in this passage is "for Jesus' sake." He Himself must be our reward.

Always being given over to death, followed by the life of Jesus being manifested, is more or less a basic pattern for Christian living, right? Death at work in me, as I lay down my life and pick up my cross, and life released to you — this brings me joy. If you embrace the same posture towards me, then together we can endure any test.

Imagine such a vertical marriage: two lives poured out for Jesus and one another, laying up eternal treasure in heaven — life-releasing death working in each spouse. In today's economy, this is the most fruitful investment of all.

Notes
1   George Whitefield to Mr. M--, London, 10 March 1753, in *A Select Collection of Letters of the Late Reverend George Whitefield, 1734-1770, Vol. III* (London, 1772), 8.

PURITY PLEDGE

One practical way that you can begin to live out your relationship for God's glory is by obeying Him in the areas of moral purity. Read the following declaration and the scriptures below. Is this something you can both commit to?

I pledge to protect your sexual purity from this day forward. I choose to respect and honor you by building up the inner person and maintaining appropriate physical boundaries.

> *For this is the will of God, your sanctification: that you abstain from sexual immorality; that each one of you know how to control his own body in holiness and honor, not in the passion of lust like the Gentiles who do not know God; that no one transgress and wrong his brother in this matter, because the Lord is an avenger in all these things, as we told you beforehand and solemnly warned you. For God has not called us for impurity, but in holiness.* (1 Thes. 4:3–7 ESV)

> *Flee from sexual immorality. Every other sin a person commits is outside the body, but the sexually immoral person sins against his own body. Or do you not know that your body is a temple of the Holy Spirit within you, whom you have from God? You are not your own, for you were bought with a price. So glorify God in your body.* (1 Cor. 6:18–20 ESV)

Honor One Another

Abstinence is essential while dating and throughout your engagement. It is, however, just one initial component of a lifelong process of keeping your marriage honorable. Consider this passage:

"Marriage is honorable among all, and the marriage bed undefiled; but forni-cators and adulterers God will judge" (Heb. 13:4).

I can recall when I was a young (immature) single Christian, how exciting I thought it would be to get married and enter into an "anything goes" free sexual experience with my wife. (Sadly, I was not a virgin when I got married. Prior to committing my life to Christ I had a typical, worldly outlook on sexuality — what is commonly referred to as a "consumer mentality." That is to say, women were coded as some sort of catalog for me to choose from for my own selfish enjoyment.) I had no preconceived evil intent, mind you, in regards to having an undefiled marriage bed, just a naive understanding of the concept. Two other translations of the verse will broaden the concept for us:

"Marriage should be honored by all, and the marriage bed kept pure, for God will judge the adulterer and all the sexually immoral" (NIV).

"Honor marriage, and guard the sacredness of sexual intimacy between wife and husband. God draws a firm line against casual and illicit sex" (THE MESSAGE).

Wow! What a shift. The verse becomes a cohesive whole. First of all, the marriage bed undefiled is a bed that is pure and sacred. Second, God draws a firm perimeter around the sin of adultery as well as all forms of sexual immorality.

To a succinct point on the undefiled bed: once you are married, you should not engage in sexual behavior that causes either of you to feel pain, disrespect, guilt, or shame. Intimacy between husband and wife is a sacred gift that should never evoke such feelings. Having the physical, emotional, and spiritual well-being of the other person in mind is essential. This is both for now and from this day forward.

Physical Boundaries

What have been the boundaries up to this point in your relationship? How well have you both done maintaining them? Is there anything that you need to repent of and apologize to your future partner about in regard to crossing boundaries?

We recommend every couple be very slow to engage in any kind of physical touch. It is a common pitfall for couples to "put the cart before the horse," as they say. The snowball rolls down the hill at breakneck speed in this arena. Lustful interaction can even seem to be sanctified when overlaid with a coating of spiritual interaction. In other words, a dating or engaged couple who pray and minister together with a bona fide anointing present, can be deceived by the spiritual intimacy into justifying and accommodating physical expression leading to the crossing of boundaries.

So, where do we begin? Every couple is a bit different and oftentimes one person in the relationship is lobbying for more physical expression. This in itself is a major red flag and should alert the other to danger. But there is no one way for everyone. For example, our niece and her future husband decided to have their first kiss at their wedding. While commendable, this is not for everyone, nor should we judge those who kiss before their wedding day.

Three things should be standard for every couple (this is not a comprehensive list):

- *An accountability relationship with a mentor couple.* This should be local and not long distance. So when you stumble and cross a boundary, you will need to be accountable to someone face-to-face.

- *An honest personal awareness of how much you can handle.* For example, holding hands may be an innocent and pure expression for one but a match that lights a fire for another! *Know yourself, then place boundaries on yourself.*

- *A commitment to get help if you are struggling in the area of sexual purity.* Sexual issues may subside for a time in the celebration of the marriage; conversely, many couples have issues come to light on the honeymoon that they never knew existed. Either way, you most likely know where you struggle, so reach out to your pastor and get hold of some helpful resources. (See Appendix G: Recommended Reading)

- *Late night curfew time and being alone in a house together.* In our opinion, these first two are "must have" boundaries. The longer the evening gets, the more temptation seems to grow; and when no one is around, no one can see. Danger lurks here!

- *Holding hands.* How can this possibly be an issue? Well, in a girl's mind it may be an innocent touch, a pure heart connect. For guys, it may be step one into a sensual area, leading to . . .

- *Arm around waist and long embraces*, aka the "full body press." To a girl this tends to be an emotional expression and feels good in that respect. To a guy, it's physical and an on-ramp towards erotic. (It may also become that for the female, but he will generally get there faster.)

- One thing leads to another, as they say, and the next natural step would be *kissing on the cheek* and/or *kissing on the lips.* (If only humans had the self-control to keep this in the "grandmother peck" category — not likely!)

- These next two are pretty obvious and should be avoided in every case: *lying next to each other* and *fondling sexual areas.*

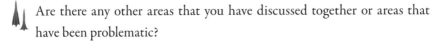 Are there any other areas that you have discussed together or areas that have been problematic?

Benefits of Staying Pure

- It is pleasing to God.

- It builds the trust that is needed for true intimacy over the years.

- It develops deeper qualities of patience and self-control.

- It affirms your future partner, showing that you care more about them than about gratifying your own desires.

- It protects you from being attacked with guilt and shame.

- It protects you from the emotional and mental trauma that can come if the relationship ends up not working out.

- It helps you to develop a stronger emotional and spiritual bond, without being distracted by the physical.

- It enables you to have a clear conscience before God.

- It increases the anticipation and enjoyment of the honeymoon.

- It is a witness to the world around you.

- It avoids bringing reproach on the name of Christ.

Which of the above benefits stirs your heart with conviction to remain pure?

PART ONE

Building a Strong Foundation

1

Covenant or Contract

Anne

It goes without saying — but I will say it anyway — the pervasive culture in the world is far from godly and seems to grow more godless every day. Marriage between a man and a woman is no longer considered the only kind of marriage, and the view of Christian marriage, in some circles, grows increasingly hostile. It is a challenge to navigate these marriage waters.

One aspect of our culture is affecting Christian marriages at an alarming rate — the misconception that marriage is a contract. Allow us to challenge you to consider and pray about having a truly biblical perspective on this subject. Our hope is not only to make you aware of this cultural pitfall but also to give you a vision of God's heart concerning your marriage.

What Types of Marriages Have You Seen?

In this broken generation I can only imagine the marriages that you have observed. Divorce and abandonment leading to fatherlessness are so common in our culture. God created us to be loved and cared for in a family. Those who grew up without this may be driven to look for love pretty much wherever they can find it. The cycle repeats itself, as this leads to further pain and brokenness. Perhaps you have been blessed to be one of the few who had parents with a God-focused marriage. In any case, the subject we are about to discuss is vital because your future marriage will reap the fruit of what your heart believes about this institution of marriage.

Let's delve a little bit into the subject of *covenant vs. contract*. Everyone has some idea of what a contract is. We make an agreement and sign a paper to prove it. Yet, we also accept that legal contracts are frequently broken. Unfortunately, this thinking has also found its way into the realm of Christian marriage. What we must realize is that marriage is *not* a contract but a *covenant!*

How Does God See Marriage?

God created marriage and to Him, marriage is sacred. In Malachi 2:14 He makes clear that those who marry enter into a covenant.

*"The Lord has been witness between you and the wife of your youth . . . she is your companion **and your wife by covenant.**"*

A covenant is "a written agreement or promise usually under seal between two or more parties especially for the performance of some action."[1] This prevalent cultural view of covenant reduces it to the level of a contract and does not truly represent the essence of covenant; it is viewed as merely legal and therefore can be dissolved by law.

Andreas Kostenberger, in his article "The Bible's Teaching on Marriage and Family," gives us a biblical definition of covenant (specifically the marriage covenant):

> A covenant is a contract between two parties that is established before God as a witness, a contract whose permanence is ultimately safeguarded by none other than God himself. In this sense, marriage is a covenant: it is entered into by the husband and the wife before God as a witness. Because it is ultimately God who has joined the marriage partners together, the husband and the wife vow to each other abiding loyalty and fidelity "till death do us part."[2]

We learn here that the two elements of covenant that distinguish it from a contract are permanence and the Chief Witness, God, who has designed that marriage is for life. Soon-to-be bride, you have chosen a dear friend to share your joy by being your witness on your wedding day. Soon-to-be groom, you have done the same. These who know and love you will sign your marriage license indicating that they have witnessed you taking your wedding vows. However, Christian weddings have an even more important Witness present; He is the

Chief Witness. Even though your friends will witness your wedding and sign the license, it is He, not they, who will hold you to your vows. In other words, although legal, a marriage union is profoundly spiritual — God is the witness of its establishment, and it is He alone who joins you together. He is also the One who expects believers to be vigilant to see their marriage covenant maintained.

It comes as no surprise that God's view of marriage is diametrically opposed to our culture's view. It is truly He, not any man, who joins the couple together: *"Therefore what God has joined together, let not man separate"* (Mk. 10:9). In other words, it was not man who joined the couple and therefore no man (or woman) can separate them. Marriage includes not only the couple who marry but also the God who unites them. A husband and wife who are believers make a commitment to view their marriage as part of God's design for their entire lives. Again, the decided difference between marriage viewed as a contract and marriage viewed as a covenant is the attitude toward permanency.

For you who are soon to marry, it is vital that you gain the heart revelation needed for permanency in your marriage. (We will discuss this in more detail in Chapter 4: Marital Vision.)

It is often said that the divorce rate in the church today is around 50 percent, or "the same as outside the church." Is this really the state of Christian marriage today? It is hard to determine. Studies yield widely different results, depending on what segment of the church is the subject. While the highest percentages are not accurate, in our experience, both personally and in the counseling room, neither are the lowest ones. For years, we have known many who have been divorced — and I venture to say that this may be your unfortunate experience as well. Although statistics may not be able to accurately ascertain the true state of marriage in the church today, one thing is sure. Malachi 2:16 tells us: *"For the LORD God of Israel says that He hates divorce, for it covers one's garment with violence."*

No matter how many Christians you may know who are divorced, you are about to enter into a covenant that is not to be broken. By His grace, never allow yourself to give consideration to divorce. Our desire is to see Christian marriages become so strong that their brightness shines out to those who do not know Christ. Ephesians 5:25 says, *"Husbands, love your wives, as Christ loved the church"* (ESV). Marriage is a picture of God's love for us. God's heart is that

Christian marriages become such a testimony to the world that the world turns to the church to discover its secret — the love, forgiveness, and grace of God.

I want to alert you to a truth that the Lord spoke to my heart: *one Christian married to another Christian will not automatically mean that their marriage will be a Christ-centered one.* Many Christians marry believing this to be true. The sad fact is that Christian marriages are failing because the marriage is not a Christ-centered one.

The single most important key to safeguarding and strengthening your marriage lies in each of you having a vital relationship with the Lord. It is consistently staying close to Him and reaching out for His grace to live pleasing to Him, that causes stability and true peace and joy to flow in your marriage. The reality is that if we are living a life satisfied in God, we will not be placing unrealistic expectations on our spouse. Rather, our love for Him can so fill us that we desire to bless our spouse instead of seeking blessing from them.

Mike and I have found that in our thirty-plus years of marriage ministry, every marriage problem we have seen is a "God problem." Either one, or both, spouses are living disconnected from the Lord. Does this mean those couples that are both connected to the Lord lead perfect lives? Of course not, but they have learned, more often than not, that when their flesh begins to rise up in selfishness they must seek to remember that God has the wisdom and the grace they need to go through — *grow* through — the challenges they are facing. It is also true of these marriages that when they have failed to apply the grace of God to a situation, humility and repentance not only restore the relationship, but actually cause it to be strengthened.

"And He said to me, 'My grace is sufficient for you, for My strength is made perfect in weakness'" (2 Cor. 12:9).

Romance and Infatuation

I want to address something that stands in the way of some maintaining their marriage covenant. It is the often-misunderstood element of romance. I think it will be helpful for you to know some of the history of romance in order to put it into its proper perspective.

Prior to Romance Coming on the Scene — an Old Testament Example

Let's observe the way marriage was approached for a few thousand years prior to the birth of Christ by looking at the beautiful story in Genesis 24 of how Isaac and Rebecca were joined together.

Abraham called his oldest servant, who ruled over all that Abraham had, and made him swear that he would find a bride for Isaac among Abraham's relatives — rather than among the Canaanites in the land where Abraham and his family lived at that time. This required that the servant travel to Abraham's homeland and find his relatives. What a challenging task this servant had! The servant had no idea how he could find this bride. He wisely turned to the Lord and made a specific request of Him so that he might be guided in this choice. We know that God was faithful to answer this prayer!

The thing that strikes me most about this story is the way Rebekah became Isaac's fiancé. Rebekah understood the servant's purpose for visiting her family's home and when asked by her family: "Will you go with this man?" her simple response was: "I will go." Think of it! She had never even seen Isaac, much less spoken to him. The only thing that she knew about Isaac was that he was a relative. Yet, she consented to leave her home, her family, and everything she had ever known, to go live in a land she had never been and enter into covenant with someone she had never even met. (Sometimes we forget that the lives we read about in Scripture were people just like you and me.)

In our culture we find this approach absolutely startling! Most decisions to marry today rely so much upon romantic emotion that to think of entering into marriage without it is totally foreign to us. (By the way, I am not suggesting that anyone should enter into marriage without it. Our belief is that initially emotional desire is a very important element in drawing two people together. However, it should by no means be the primary reason for marriage. On the other hand, our experience counseling couples who married without this element — basing their decision solely upon prophetic words or a sense that the Lord told them to — is that this resulted in significant issues in the marriage.)

The compelling thing, and my point for using the story of Isaac and Rebekah, is that although, as far as we know, romance was lacking for Rebekah, covenant was not. Covenant was very important to our spiritual forefathers. Hopefully Rebekah was able to enjoy romantic emotions, yet even if she did not, she was committed to her marriage covenant no matter what — and she pleased and honored her God in the process.

Romance through History

In millennia past, marriages were arranged — as illustrated by Isaac and Rebekah's story. Abraham's purpose for arranging Isaac's bride the way he did was spiritual. He desired that Isaac not marry a Canaanite but one who also followed the true God. However, throughout history parents arranged their child's marriage for a variety of other purposes — mainly financial, positional, or political.

Although love was often referred to in connection with marriage, it was the Romantic poets (mid-seventeenth century until the close of the eighteenth century) who actually brought romantic love to the forefront to the degree that it became expected. The Victorian era ushered in the idea that romantic love should be considered when choosing a marriage partner. Today it is the main focus for many in their choice of a marriage partner.

Today: What About Romance and You?

You are in the wonderful season of engagement and no doubt enjoying the blessing of the emotions that the Lord has given you for your future spouse. I want to share something here that may not be welcome news, yet is so important for you to know in order to help you navigate this marriage covenant you are about to enter into.

Wisdom demands that romantic emotions should not be the major factor in your decision to marry. Why do I say this? A doctor of psychology explains the chemical elements of these emotions:

> When we are attracted to someone we think has potential as a mate, levels of two brain chemicals go up – dopamine and norepinephrine, and a third chemical decreases serotonin. This is what causes all of the symptoms of infatuation . . . Your brain sets you up to be hyper-focused on what you like about this one person and to discount or ignore the parts you don't like, in order to facilitate the 'getting together' part of the mating process. The infatuation state can last 18–24 months. You

may still be in the infatuation stage up until the time you get married, depending on how long you have been together.[3]

So you see, although these romantic emotions (infatuation) are a blessing, they are definitely not, as stated earlier, a rock that marriage should be built upon. When we were courting, the Lord began teaching me concerning the subject of infatuation.

Mike and I were out for one of our frequent walks around our Bible school campus when I came to a horrifying revelation! I looked at him and suddenly discovered that I was not experiencing any romantic feelings for him at all in that moment. They had been there and then . . . poof! They vanished!

The absence of these feelings caused me some alarm. In my immaturity I remember thinking, "Oh, my goodness, maybe he is not the right one after all!" Without me realizing it, the attitude of the culture had infiltrated my mind — I really believed that this was a serious problem for our relationship! The Lord did restore the romantic emotions to me but not without first teaching me a very valuable lesson: as history, the biblical account of Rebekah, and even science teaches us, romantic emotions are not the major element upon which a marriage relationship should be built.

I am so thankful that He allowed me to experience this during our courtship. He was awakening me to the truth about the fickleness of romantic emotions. I was being taught that it is natural for these feelings to ebb and flow, and that a marriage cannot be built on the shaky foundation of infatuation. If we are not aware of this in marriage, when these emotions do wane, we can become disillusioned. This can bring a temptation to believe the lie that we have married the wrong person and should possibly consider divorce so that we can find the "right" person.

Once the initial stage of infatuation ends, it does not mean that you will never experience any romantic emotions in your marriage relationship. However, be aware that *they will dissipate and this should not be a concern for you.* What will remain is the covenant that you made with your spouse on your wedding day. What will also remain is the amazing opportunity for you to forge a mature, deep, and lasting love as you allow the Holy Spirit to work in your lives, shaping you more and more into His image in your union.

It is so important to the health of your marriage that you allow the Holy Spirit to fill your heart with His truth concerning your covenant. Be alert to how the culture may attempt to pull you in its direction. Be steadfast and firm. The covenant you will soon make is one that is meant to stand upon the foundation of God's design for marriage. His design is permanency. He will be the Chief Witness on your special day; reminding yourself of this truth throughout your marriage will help you to "fight the good fight of faith" (1 Tim. 6:12) and strengthen your marriage in the process.

DISCUSS TOGETHER

1. What are the main differences between the culture's view of contract and God's view of covenant in marriage?

2. What practical elements will you include in your marriage to assure that you are living God's view of covenant?

3. What role are emotions presently playing in your relationship? Do you need a shift in your thinking?

4. Discuss your reaction to what psychologists say concerning the brevity of romantic emotions in marriage.

Love and Loyalty

Mike

Somewhere in my early Christian life, I heard teaching on the principles of covenant — the absolute faithfulness of God toward me. This has encouraged me in my faith and taught me much about loyalty in relationships — God toward me and me toward others.

Covenant is an expression of the attributes of God. He declared himself to Moses on Mount Sinai, saying, *"The LORD, the LORD, the compassionate and gracious God, slow to anger, abounding in love and faithfulness, maintaining love to thousands, and forgiving wickedness, rebellion and sin"* (Ex. 34:6–7 NIV).

God's covenant is overflowing with his affection toward us.

The LORD did not set his affection on you and choose you because you were more numerous than other peoples, for you were the fewest of all peoples. But it was because the LORD loved you and kept the oath he swore to your ancestors that he brought you out with a mighty hand and redeemed you from the land of slavery, from the power of Pharaoh king of Egypt. Know therefore that the LORD your God is God; he is the faithful God, keeping his covenant of love to a thousand generations of those who love him and keep his commandments. (Deut. 7:7–9 NIV)

God had made covenant with Abram some five hundred years earlier. God doesn't love based on feelings but based on covenant. The New Testament counterpart to this can be found in the "love chapter," First Corinthians 13.

Love is patient, love is kind. It does not envy, it does not boast, it is not proud. It does not dishonor others, it is not self-seeking, it is not easily angered, it keeps no record of wrongs. Love does not delight in evil but rejoices with the truth. It always protects, always trusts, always hopes, always perseveres. Love never fails. (vv. 4–8 NIV)

This is the God kind of love, "agape," to which we are to aspire in all of our relationships — faithful, covenant love. Jesus Christ is the covenant maker. This forever agreement is between him and Father God.

And it was not without an oath! Others became priests without any oath, but he became a priest with an oath when God said to him: "The Lord has sworn and will not change his mind: 'you are a priest forever.'" Because of this oath, Jesus has become the guarantor of a better covenant. (Heb. 7:20–22 NIV)

There will be times in life when we don't "feel" like God is near. Our faith however, has an unwavering core, deep on the inside, where we know that He will never leave us or forsake us. It's just who God is: Father, Son, and Holy Spirit with whom we have an unbreakable bond. God's covenant vow to us is what enables us, surrounded by such a guarantee, to approach the marriage altar to pledge an unbreakable bond with another person. Unless Christ returns to earth in your lifetime, the joining together of a man and a woman in marriage is "till death do us part." This is covenant.

Learning marriage skills is no doubt essential in any marriage. However, if you want your marriage to survive and soar over the long haul, you must embrace the meaning of covenant. Is happiness a part of covenant? Absolutely! But *happiness is an inside job and is fueled by the unselfish acts of covenant day in and day out in a marriage.*

Dangers of a Contract Mentality

Imagine if God related to us on the basis of "contract." This is an agreement between two parties, totally dependent on performance of all that is stated in the agreement. God gives me all the promises from His Word, and I in turn agree to obey Him and live my life according to His requirements. If either party fails to comply, the contract is nullified. That is scary! Thankfully, we are in covenant, which is an irrevocable commitment valid at least until death and is not dependent upon the performance of either party. This is a true definition of the marriage union.

As couples have adopted the idea that marriage is a contract agreement, the prevalence of divorce in our nation has skyrocketed. Divorce rates went from 3 percent in 1867 to 50 percent in 1985.[4] A significant increase occurred after 1969, when the concept of "no-fault" divorce began to be encoded in state laws. While adultery or extreme cruelty were formerly the legal grounds for dissolution, it is now deemed sufficient grounds if both parties simply no longer agree to be married. This was a blatant shift from *covenant* to *contract* mentality, and it took its toll. In recent years, even the idea of contract marriage is waning — more couples are living together with no agreement at all, nothing binding them to stay together — and with it society's core understanding of marriage has disappeared, so that even its natural characteristics have now been redefined by governments.

Without the umbrella of covenant, there is a lack of protection. A marriage based on a contract mentality does not offer a very secure covering for the family. Craig Hill of Family Foundations International conveys the impact on children: "If the message presented between the parents is that of contract, 'If you make me unhappy or don't measure up, I'm going to leave you and find somebody else,' the heart of the child thinks, 'I wonder what will happen to me if "I" make him/her unhappy and don't measure up?' In the heart, this feeling is naturally next transferred to God."[5]

A healthy marriage is the key to a healthy family. In Genesis 12:3 the promise is made to Abram: *"In you all the families of the earth shall be blessed."* The blessing of God is released through families, and the core of the family is the marriage that gave it birth. The day-to-day ways in which we were defined by family are many times the culprit behind the lies we believe as adults. The enemy's plan: attack the marriage to hurt the family and hinder the blessing. God's plan: protect the marriage to strengthen the family and release the blessing.

Marriage as a Prophetic Portrait

Marriage is a prophetic picture of Christ and the church, God and His people. I believe that the devil hates marriage with a passion similar to how he hates Israel. Knowing the obvious, his venom is aimed at keeping the Promised Land from seeing its prophetic destiny fulfilled, namely, the return of Jesus to set up His government in the age to come, in that very location. Likewise, the Christian marriage covenant is meant to demonstrate the covenant relationship between God and His people. A healthy and growing Christian marriage is a solid witness to the gospel. Broken marriages in the church are not helpful when an unbeliever is vetting God. The world is watching and taking note of how we the church are living out our marriages. Gary Thomas points out in his masterpiece, *Sacred Marriage*, "As long as a couple is married, they continue to display — however imperfectly — the ongoing commitment between Christ and his church."[6]

One of the most widely used passages of Scripture in weddings is Ephesians 5. It talks of submitting to one another in the fear of the Lord, husbands being the head of the wife as Christ is the head of the church, and husbands loving their own wives in the same manner in which Christ loved the church. It also speaks of our being members of Christ's body, of His flesh and of His bones, and the glory of a man and woman becoming one flesh. In concluding the chapter, Paul says: *"This is a great mystery, but I speak concerning Christ and the church"* (v. 32).

Any godly character that my marriage might display is essentially drawn from this heavenly partnership of God with His people. From the Garden to the Apocalypse the pattern is clear — our earthly marriages must glean from how

God interacts with His beloved bride. Earthly marriage was established by God in the image of His own eternal marriage with His people.

DISCUSS TOGETHER

Write your own definition of covenant.

Notes

1 *Webster's New Collegiate Dictionary*, 1974, s.v. "covenant."

2 Andreas J. Kostenberger, *The Bible's Teaching on Marriage and the Family* (Washington, D.C.: Family Research Council, 2011).

3 Deborah Anderson, "Preserving the Passion in Your Relationship: How the Biology of Love Can Affect Your Marriage," *Inside Weddings*, https://www.insideweddings.com/news/expert-advice/preserving-the-passion-in-your-relationship/1567/ (accessed June 9, 2015).

4 U.S. Department of Health, Education & Welfare, "100 Years of Marriage & Divorce Statistics in the United States, 1867-1967," Alexander A. Plateris, Publication #74-1902, Rockville, MD, U.S. Government Printing Office, 1973.

5 Craig Hill, *Marriage: Covenant or Contract*, Kindle Edition, (Littleton, CO: Family Foundations International, 2011).

6 Gary L. Thomas, *Sacred Marriage: What if God Designed Marriage to Make Us Holy More Than to Make Us Happy*, (Grand Rapids: Zondervan, 2000), 31.

2

Let's Build a Marriage

Mike

There are two ways to build a marriage. One is to hear what the Lord is saying and to obey. The result will be a wise couple with a marriage built on solid rock. When the storms come, this marriage will stand firm. The other alternative is to hear what the Lord is saying but not put it into practice, or worse yet, to not even be seeking to hear Him at all. The result will be a foolish couple with a marriage built on shifting sand. When the storms come, this marriage will be liable to a fall.

When Jesus appeared to John at the end of the first century to give a message to the seven churches, the emphasis was, "He who has an ear, let him hear what the Spirit says" (Rev. 2:7). *Marriages that hear and obey will be full of light, and marriages full of light will overcome darkness.*

Walking Side by Side

Here's the scene on the Emmaus road: two disciples walking together on a journey with Jesus coming alongside and speaking to them. Can we not see an image of marriage in this scenario? As a matter of fact, as I ponder our many occasions of counseling a married couple, the bull's-eye that I'm usually aiming for is: "What do you feel the Lord is saying to you individually and corporately?" **Single or married, our greatest asset will always be found in hearing what the Spirit is saying.** To say it another way: *recognition is your best ally.* This is a solid marriage principle and also one of several good litmus tests for singles as they evaluate a potential mate. Is the person you plan to spend the rest of your life with attentive to the Lord's voice?

A person's history carries on into their marriage. Although the marriage ceremony contains a covenant promise, we need more than promises before we commit to a "till death do us part" relationship. We need to have a proven track record that transcends romance and all of the putting our best foot forward that transpires during courtship. I've seen too many tragedies of "missionary dating" gone south when the promises made were barely an inch deep and birthed out of infatuation or desperation to marry.

Know the history of your potential mate-to-be. Have they heard from God; are they hearing from God; and do you trust that they *will* hear from God when the added responsibility of marriage is placed upon them? It's not perfection that we seek, only consistency.

In the Emmaus Road story, both disciples walked with Jesus and received revelation at the same time. Seasons of joint growth are the most pleasant in a marriage. *The testing comes when one heart burns and the other does not; when one set of eyes are opened and the other remains veiled.* [1]

"Then their eyes were opened, and they knew Him; and He vanished from their sight. And they said one to another, 'Did not our heart burn within us, while He talked with us on the road, and while He opened the Scriptures to us?'" (Lk. 24:31–32). Each spouse having their eyes open and then being transparent with one another — this is the posture of strength every couple needs. Stay humble, stay open, and your marriage will endure. The spiritual-growth orbit of husband and wife will not match exactly, of course, but they should at least be close.

The most encouraging part of the Emmaus account is that after the recognition was birthed they remembered when it was conceived: "Hey, now that I think of it, my heart was burning inside of me when Jesus was talking to us." (My paraphrase of Luke 24:32.) We want this experience to take place repeatedly over the course of our married lives. It's called **building a history in God.**

Your single life will continue on into your marriage. Yes, you will be one flesh and you'll possibly even have a name change (ladies), but YOU will still be YOU. Your relationship with God will not lose its continuity; the transition is one of single disciple to married disciple. Each spouse staying on track with a single devotion to Christ, will solidify the threefold cord. *"Though one may be overpowered by another, two can withstand him. And a threefold cord is not quickly broken"* Eccl. 4:12).

Leaving and Cleaving

*"Therefore shall a man leave his father and his mother and shall **cleave** unto his wife, and they shall be one flesh."* (Gen. 2:24 KJV)

*"My soul **clings** to You; Your right hand upholds me."* (Ps. 63:8 NASB)

*"There is a friend who sticks **closer** than a brother."* (Prov. 18:24 NASB)

Cleaving, clinging, and *closeness,* all from the same Hebrew root word, convey a strong attachment.[2] In the beginning of our lives we are as close to our mothers as one can get; we are attached in every way. Ideally, this attachment extends to a father, then to siblings, to covenant friends, and most of all to God Himself. A parent-child relationship is a covenant one.

I continue to love my three children (in their thirties at this writing) and am still cognizant of the covenant bond between us. We did our best to wean them from dependency on us toward a covenant relationship with God. We did not lose them; they simply transitioned.

I can recall in my own life the ascension into a higher covenant bond as Anne and I were married. I left my parents, she left hers, and she became my new, number-one, highest-priority covenant relationship. I did not lose the other relationships, but this one superseded them. I haven't stopped cleaving to this very day as I write these words. Marriage is the highest covenant commitment, other than with God, that one can ever enter into. Sealed with vows and rings at the launch, one must choose with ongoing intention to nurture the bond. When my son got married I experienced this process from a new vantage point. I literally had a front row seat, being the officiant of the wedding! I tearfully led them into their covenant pledges and into the future glorious mystery of the one-flesh union. One person adhering to another — this is the essence of cleaving.

You cannot cleave without leaving. It can be difficult, though, to find the right balance. In the next chapter we will consider expectations that you will carry into your married life. Among them will be the frequency of relating with friends and family. I guarantee this will save an argument or two if talked through ahead of time. I am "leaving" my best friends and family behind to enter into this paramount relationship with my future covenant partner. What about all the great things God has done through these people? Will we still retain those friends? Will we still relate to our natural families? Yes, but in a different way. We retain our community and need its support, yet in the midst are to honor and esteem our spouse above all others.

"*Therefore a man shall leave his father and mother and be joined to his wife, and they shall become one flesh*" (Gen. 2:24). Jesus quoted this verse in Matthew 19, and added these words: "*Therefore what God has joined together, let not man separate*" (v. 6). The premarital process is unto this glorious combining of two lives. Thus the preparation must be as comprehensive as can be, laying the foundation for greater ongoing depths of partnership throughout the marriage.

We normally use the word *baggage* to describe negative attributes in a person, but may I say that I am thankful for the positive "baggage" my wife and I brought to our marriage. Though both sets of parents had troubled marriages, they passed much good to us — values and life principles, which we carried into our new relationship. An important asset in marriage is to be cognizant of these blessings while also being aware of areas of life that were negatively modeled and taught.

When you and your spouse establish a brand new home you aren't really starting with a clean slate. The prevailing attitudes of your parents formed your own basic attitude toward yourself. While we are thankful for the positive fruit, we must be determined to remove the negative. Transformation is our goal, replacing any ungodly attitudes with what the Word of God says. Peter Scazzero, author of *Emotionally Healthy Spirituality*, describes this well:

> Our families are the most powerful group to which we will ever belong … God's desire for us to leave our families is similar to the desire he had for the Israelites to leave Egypt. Although the Israelites did physically leave the land of Egypt, a great deal of Egyptian culture and thinking remained in them.[3]

It is essential that each spouse do the work of going back to heal whatever hinders forward momentum in the marriage. If past pain is affecting my marriage in the present, then it's present pain. *The Life Model: Living From the Heart Jesus Gave You* discusses the necessity of healing in order that strong love bonds can be created: "Pain from the past cannot stay in the past, until it receives healing."[4] This is actually a part of the leaving process, which continues after the wedding, by the way. Failure to connect the dots of our history will result in a disconnected spirituality. We cannot afford to be disconnected from ourselves, much less our spouse.

On a practical note, how much of my past life do I need to share with my spouse? I desire emotional intimacy at a deep level, but I'm concerned that some parts of my past might hinder more than unify. Ephesians 4:29 is a good filter on the front end to sift the words that we are considering sharing with our spouse:

> *"Let no corrupt word proceed out of your mouth, but what is good for necessary edification, that it may impart grace to the hearers."*

Other verses also point us toward the emphasis on the positive.

> *"Therefore, if anyone is in Christ, he is a new creation; old things have passed away; behold, all things have become new."* (2 Cor. 5:17)

> *"Set your mind on things above, not on things on the earth."* (Col. 3:2)

> *"There is therefore now no condemnation to those who are in Christ Jesus, who do not walk according to the flesh, but according to the Spirit."* (Rom. 8:1)

The debased details of our past (memories that reek of decay) are not to be shared with our spouse nor remembered in our own history. On the one hand, premarital preparation should be that fine-tooth comb that goes deep and probes the contents of one's history. Before I commit to one person for the rest of my earthly life, I need to know as much as possible of their character and its origin. On the other hand, we need wisdom to know how to tell the truth and testify to God's work in our lives, without defiling or damaging the hearer. While much can be accomplished in the normal course of friendship building, we recommend a mature counselor or couple to facilitate and help you sort out your past experiences and how they will blend into your marriage. I like this guideline from Joe Beam, founder of Family Dynamics Institute:

> Only if the three following conditions are satisfied is it okay not to tell: 1) you are confident that what happened does not stand as a barrier to intimacy in your marriage, 2) it would harm, rather than benefit your spouse to know, and 3) you tell no lie to your spouse. Even if the first two criteria are met and your spouse asks . . . always tell the truth.[5]

We have occasionally counseled couples to hit pause on their planned wedding trajectory, based on knowledge that surfaced in the counseling. True, past sins and failures are under the blood of the Lamb, but has maturity been established? We may not have transgressed in a particular area for years but also not gone very far into significant growth in that same area. Barely maintaining freedom is not sufficient foundation for the weighty alliance of marriage.

DISCUSS TOGETHER

1. What is your understanding of leaving your parents?
2. What does cleaving mean?
3. What are some common ways that a couple might fail to "cut the cord" from Mom and Dad?

Leaving the negative past behind is an essential step in the cleaving of marriage. We still remain committed to honor our parents and all they built into our past that was beautiful, but are about to transfer allegiance and loyalty to one primary person.

Kindred Hearts

While He was still talking to the multitudes, behold, His mother and brothers stood outside, seeking to speak with Him. Then one said to Him, "Look, Your mother and your brothers are standing outside, seeking to speak with you." But He answered and said to the one who told Him, "Who is My mother, and who are My brothers?" And He stretched out His hand toward His disciples and said, "Here are My mother and My brothers! For whoever does the will of My Father in heaven is My brother and sister and mother." (Mt. 12:46-50)

Jesus speaks of the preeminence of spiritual relationships. Luke says it this way: *"My mother and brothers are those who hear God's word and put it into practice"* (Lk. 8:21 NIV). Most Christians have an inner circle of friends with kindred hearts after God. It's disturbing to see a husband or a wife whose spouse is not in that circle.

Those Emmaus Road walks are critical. Long spiritual discourse was the brick and mortar of Anne's and my dating and courtship. It is what we built on and still build on today. *Every well I dig in my spiritual life provides a drink for my spouse.* Some wells we dig together, some separately. Discovering, hearing, and doing: these are activities that make us family, with God and with one another.

Jesus clearly identified doing the will of His Father as a powerful component of connection. The word *obedience* works well here. As I seek to obey God and overcome whatever gets in the way, I am drawn closer to Him. I am blessed to be married to a woman who shares my passion in this regard. She is one who *delights to defer* to the Lord.

Our beautiful example is Jesus: *"Though He was a Son, yet He learned obedience by the things which He suffered. And having been perfected, He became the author of eternal salvation to all who obey Him"* (Heb. 5:8–9). A concept I learned long ago: when I embrace this process and its ongoing development, I become a source of life to those around me. Husbands obey; do the will of God. Wives obey; do the will of God. And, I might add, be patient with one another on the learning curve. When both of you are obeying God together, the vertical focus of your marriage will actually knit your kindred hearts ever more closely to one another.

Living life is meant to be unto the glory of God (see First Corinthians 10:31). If I'm single I live for His glory; if I'm married I live for His glory. The greatest thing you and your future partner can aspire to do is to build a marriage for the glory of God. It will produce fruit that remains, that lasts for an eternity.

Notes
1 Mike Rizzo, *Longing for Eden: Embracing God's Vision in Your Marriage* (Create Space, 2012), 50.
2 Brown-Driver-Briggs Hebrew and English Lexicon, Unabridged, Electronic Database. Copyright 2002, 2003, 2006 by Biblesoft, Inc. All rights reserved. Used by permission. BibleSoft.com
3 Peter Scazzero, *Emotionally Healthy Spirituality*, (Nashville: Thomas Nelson, 2006), 95, 100.
4 James G. Friesen and others, *The Life Model: Living From the Heart Jesus Gave You* (Pasadena: Shepherd's House, 2000), 18.
5 Joe Beam, *Becoming One* (West Monroe, LA: Howard Publishing, 1999), 108.

3

Evaluating the Relationship

Mike

Compatibility

The majority of couples consist of complementary partners; that is to say, opposites attract. I'm so thankful that I didn't marry a woman with exactly the same personality as myself. I have appreciated the balance brought into my life as a result of living with someone unlike me. My wife agrees on this point. We have gleaned much from one another's contrasting temperaments. There is, however, a sameness, a rapport, that a couple must have in certain foundational areas. Consider the following four areas of compatibility given by author Gary Thomas in his book *Sacred Search*:[1]

1. *Spiritual Compatibility.* We've already mentioned the essential attribute of seeking to build a marriage for the glory of God. You must have the shared spiritual value system that encompasses Matthew 6:33 — seek first the kingdom of God.

2. *Relational Compatibility.* Hopefully, if you've come this far in a relationship that you want to marry someone, you share an appreciation for one another's personality and character. Who we are relating to during engagement will be the same person we will relate to on the honeymoon and on into years of marriage. You need to like each other *now* and not be banking on the potential that you see developing. *"Marry someone you want to be married*

*to for the rest of your life, not someone you hope to transform into a
satisfactory spouse in five years' time."²*

3. *Recreational Compatibility.* My wife and I have different interests
   but also many that are similar. Chances are that if you had zero
   interests in common, you would not have gone this far in the
   relationship. It's still wise, however, to discuss this area because you
   will spend a lot of time together in marriage. Who knows, you may
   even acquire some of your future spouse's interests.

4. *Environmental Compatibility.* This is pretty clear-cut, but many
   couples have failed to discuss the possibilities that might lie ahead.
   Are there any deal breakers for you — regions of the country or
   overseas that you absolutely could not live in?

Before we work through lists of questions and expectations that will help
determine compatibility, let us prayerfully consider if there are any red flags.

⟶ CAUTION FLAGS ⟵

The need for caution may not necessarily mean that you shouldn't marry
each other, but it may indicate the need to slow down the relationship. As you
will see in the next chapter, a primary objective in marriage is to have a vision
for ongoing spiritual growth and character transformation. This vision, in its
beginning stages, should already be in place in your relationship. If it is, then
you've been honest about areas needing to change in your personal life and how
you can make progress together as a team. Whatever is manifesting in your relationship now, will increase in intensity after marriage.

 Read the following list. Are there any caution flags in your relationship?

1. Uneasy gut feeling that something is wrong in our relationship.
2. Frequent arguments.
3. Jealousy or irrational anger when one of us interacts with someone
   of the opposite sex.
4. Apprehension discussing certain subjects because we are afraid of
   the reaction.
5. Extreme emotional expressions; unpredictable mood swings.

6. Controlling behavior — I feel like I'm being manipulated.

7. Feeling trapped — not wanting to hurt each other by even suggesting that marriage may not be for us.

8. Lack of respect — I'm constantly being criticized and treated with sarcasm.

9. Lack of personal responsibility — my fiancé struggles to hold down a job and pay bills.

10. Pride — he/she has difficulty admitting when wrong, thus we never fully resolve conflict.

11. Dependent on parents for emotional and financial security.

12. History of failed dating relationships.

13. Addictions — do either of you struggle with alcohol, drugs, or porn? If you struggled in the past, how long have you been free?

14. Selfishness — overly self-centered, always wants their own way, tends towards narcissism.

15. Bad habits — yes we all have some, but are there any major trouble spots? Are there any pet peeves that drive you crazy?

Strengths & Weaknesses

List five areas that you each feel you are strong in and five areas in which you are weak. Discuss your answers with each other. Note: your future spouse may want to add some strengths for you or lovingly point out a weakness you missed.

Strengths   *Weaknesses*

1. _____   1. _____

2. _____   2. _____

3. _____   3. _____

4. _____   4. _____

5. _____   5. _____

DISCUSS TOGETHER

In the next two sections, answer the questions individually, discuss with one another, and then share your results with your premarital counselor.

Relational History

1. What brought you two together? What led to this point of wanting to get married?

2. Are you Christians? Is Jesus Christ the Lord of your lives?

3. Are you active members of a church?

4. Do you have your parents' permission, support, and blessing?

5. Describe any serious dating relationships that you have had in the past. Briefly tell how they began, progressed, and ended.

6. Have you previously been married? How long ago was your divorce, and why did the marriage end?

Expectations

We all have expectations, often ones we're not even aware of. It's important to know what these are, since they affect our feelings and reactions on a deep level. The goal is to discover possible areas of conflict now instead of later. Go through the list and simply give a minute of thought to each question. Share your answers with each other and your premarital counselor. Some questions will provoke more conversation than others.

1. Where would you like to live? In what setting? (City, suburbs, country, etc.)

2. How much individual, personal time do you anticipate needing each week?

3. How often do you expect to spend time with your friends after you are married?

4. How will you relate to opposite-sex friends?

5. How socially active do you plan to be as a couple?

6. Are you planning a job change after marriage?

7. How many hours of sleep do you generally need? Are you a morning or evening person?

8. Are family meal times important to you? How often will you eat out?

9. Will you have a regular date night?

10. What kind of entertaining will you do, and how often?

11. Do you have similar interests in media? (Watching movies, playing video games, browsing the Internet, etc.)

12. What recreational activities will you pursue together? Individually?

13. Do you have any favorite vacation activities?

14. How do you feel about drinking alcoholic beverages or having them in your home?

15. Who will do most of the cooking and of what types of food?

16. Can you predict how you will work together in these areas of household responsibilities? Laundry, cleaning the kitchen, cleaning bathrooms, making the bed, taking out the trash, home repairs, yard work, grocery shopping, interior decorating, pet care, car maintenance, planning the social calendar.

17. Do you plan to have children? If so, how many? When will you begin?

18. What is your view on birth control? (See Appendix A.)

19. With what frequency do you plan to visit extended family? (His parents / her parents.)

20. Where will you spend holidays such as Christmas and Thanksgiving?

21. How do you think your relationship with your parents will change after you are married?

Notes
1 Gary Thomas, *Sacred Search,* (Colorado Springs: David C. Cook, 2013).
2 Ibid., 161.

PART TWO

A Unique Partnership

4

Marital Vision

Anne

"Where there is no prophetic vision the people cast off restraint."
Proverbs 29:18 ESV

"If people can't see what God is doing, they stumble all over themselves".
Proverbs 29:18 THE MESSAGE

Proverbs 29:18 magnifies the importance of vision in our lives. Having vision for your life and for your marriage is of vital importance. For many of us the word *vision* brings to mind the subject of life calling. We may also use it in the context of a specific assignment that the Lord has called us to for a season.

While these are accurate uses of the word, its practical expression is broader. The word translated *vision* here more specifically translates, "the revelation of divine truth." I like to put it this way: *vision is God speaking to us about Himself — and about our relationship with Him and His kingdom.*

As believers in the Lord Jesus Christ, I think you would agree that it is wisdom to live in the purposes God has for us. If we are honest with ourselves, we'll admit that we really don't fully know what these are (although, at times, we may think we do). Only the One who created each of us so uniquely knows what is best for each unique one He has created.

We either live in the "divine revelation of truth," or we live without it. Have you ever considered the importance of the words of Proverbs 29:18? Clearly, if we lack vision, we are susceptible to "casting off restraint" or "stumbling all over ourselves." This sounds a bit precarious to me. I don't believe that any of us want to live in this place.

Let's begin by discussing the life foundation that we each need in order to receive vision. Then we will look at the three areas of marital vision we must build upon this foundation in order to have the fullness in marriage the Lord intends for us.

Vision's Foundation

The foundation for your life and all vision is found in your relationship with the Lord. Now this may seem like an "of course!" (or, to use the vernacular, a "duh!" moment), but please bear with me. There is an important reason to focus on this for a while — its absolute necessity to the life of your coming marriage.

What kind of relationship do you presently have with Him? Is it a casual, occasional one, or would you say it is more characterized by a consistent deliberateness resulting in a deepening connection with Him? Is He central in your life, or is He peripheral? The centrality of Christ in your life will determine the health of your coming marriage; only He can give you the love for your spouse that a godly marriage requires.

Think back over your dating/courting season. How did you come to the place of deciding to marry? Wasn't it because you were both desirous and deliberate about pursuing your relationship? I would venture to say that you spent lots of time together talking and getting to know each other, right? Your relationship took time and effort to develop and so, too, does our relationship with the Lord. We must be willing to invest time to come before Him, so we can pursue getting to know Him and His plans for us.

Psalm 37:23–24 tells us: *"The steps of a good man are ordered by the LORD, and He delights in his way. Though he fall, he shall not be utterly cast down; for the LORD upholds him with His hand."*

Adam Clarke's 1831 commentary on Psalm 37 states: "When his steps are ordered by the Lord, He delighteth in his way, because it is that into which His own good Spirit has directed him." How wonderful to live a life directed by the Lord and in a way that delights Him. In order be directed by God's "own good Spirit," however, we must be in consistent communication with Him. In this place of nearness we are promised that when we do make a mistake and begin to fall, He is there to hold us up. In other words, He will speak if we are listening.

Perhaps when you were a child you had a parent who taught you how to ride a bike. Your mom or dad encouraged you and stayed right with you as you began to ride without them holding on. Yet, they stayed close enough so that if you were to tip and begin to fall they were there to catch you and hold you up. In order for your parent to be able to do this, you could not speed ahead of them but needed to stay in close proximity.

Are you in a place in your relationship with Him where you can be directed by Him and upheld "with His hand"? If not, are you desirous of this close relationship with Him? If you find the desire to meet with the Lord in the secret place lacking, or perhaps just not strong enough to motivate you, ask Him for this desire. Ask Him to increase your hunger for Him.

In my own personal life (I think this is true of human nature), I find that this hunger is born out of the revelation — leading to desperation — that I can do NOTHING without Him. I am so thankful that, in His kindness and mercy, He has caused me to be aware of this. An intimate relationship with Him grows as we have what Adam Clarke calls "a violent earnestness" for it.

Matthew 11:12 says, *"And from the days of John the Baptist until now the kingdom of heaven suffers violence, and the violent take it by force"* (KJV). We "take" the kingdom as we are "violent" with prioritizing time to seek God as well as determinedly giving reign to the Holy Spirit to rule over our flesh. Why am I placing such emphasis on this in a premarriage manual? I made reference to it earlier; the life of your marriage depends upon how you live out your relationship with Him. You can try to coast through your marriage living life the best way *you* know how, but believe me, you definitely will not coast in a pleasant manner — it may feel more like a very bumpy ride. The alternate, and preferable way to do life in your marriage is for you to regularly pause, meet with, and stay connected to the Source of life.

In our thirty-plus years of marriage counseling, the single most common issue in every marriage we have encountered is that either one or both spouses lack a heart connection with the Lord. What do I mean by heart connection? A heart connection is what happens when we consistently come before Him and His Word with a heart that is open to what He wants to say to us. As we do this, little by little we gain more heart knowledge of who He is and how very much He loves us. This fuels our hearts to want more. This knowledge opens us to have an ear to hear what He is saying and results in a desire to be willing to take His grace to obey.

A beautiful truth of His kingdom is found in Second Corinthians 12:9, "*My strength is made perfect in weakness.*" If we are willing to humble ourselves, admit our frailty, and give Him our weakness, He will make the divine exchange; He will give us His strength.

The amazing fruit of living like this is that we live satisfied in our relationship with the Lord. When we live satisfied in Him we will not be placing unrealistic demands upon our spouse. Rather, we will find ourselves filled with Him, and the result will be an overflow of His life out to our spouse. When both spouses live filled with Him, it results in the best marriage they could ever imagine.

Now that we have established the foundation for marriage, let's talk about three specific aspects of vision that should be set upon this foundation. As you have discussed and planned for your future together, have these found their way into your conversations? If not, now is the time to consider them and establish together their importance for your marriage. These truly are necessary to build a lasting, godly marriage.

One: Destiny and Calling

The first area of vision in marriage is a sense of calling or destiny the Lord places on each couple. The outworking of our relationship with Him will bring recognition of what His heart is for our individual destiny. It is here, in nearness to Him, that we find fueling for the details of His assignment for us in any particular season.

As you prepare to marry I hope that you have already learned what your future spouse feels the Lord calling them to and have prayerfully considered if your callings are similar enough to marry. Although it is not necessary that both husband and wife have identical callings, compatibility of callings is very important.

I want to share our experience in this area. Mike and I met in Bible school. Mike had already been serving on the mission field for two years prior to coming to Bible school and was looking for a woman to be his wife who would be willing to return to the field with him. He put this before the Lord, and as he considered pursuing me needed to know where I stood. I had gone to Bible school sensing in my heart that perhaps the Lord was calling me to a foreign field of service. Through a series of events that I will not take the time to share, Mike learned that I did, indeed, feel a similar calling and would be excited to return with him as his life partner.

Even though you may not feel called primarily to the same thing, you are called to share some aspect of vision together. What has the Lord put in your hearts? Perhaps it is a vision to share in ministry together, or begin a business. It may be that you feel called to raise godly children (biological, adopted, or both). The calling on each marriage is unique and flows out of *the coming together of two individuals uniquely created by God.*

Whatever your vision is — whatever the Lord has called you to do — recognize that, in His eyes, the two of you will be harnessed together for His kingdom. What does this mean? If God has led you to join your lives together, it is for His purposes. Walking these out will be another way you demonstrate His lordship over your lives. As a single person you have already prayed, "'Your kingdom come, Your will be done' in my life." As the Lord joins you together in marriage, it is for the purpose of His kingdom coming and His will being done through your lives together, as well as individually. Having been privileged to come alongside many marriages, we can say that a couple that has this concept at the heart of their marriage will have a marriage that is both powerful and beautiful at the same time; no matter the challenges they face, they choose to do that which will ultimately bring glory to their Lord and King.

Knowing that He has a unique destiny for your marriage will energize you and help to solidify your purpose and commitment to each other. You will also discover that there is great joy in flowing together in what He has marked you for as a couple.

Two: Longevity or Permanency

The second aspect of marital vision is longevity — or permanency — in your marriage. It will be of great value to you to be alert to the fact that many marriages you have seen, both in and out of the church, do not hold to the sacred truth that marriage was intended to be "until death do us part." You must remember that just because so many marriages have ended in divorce, it will never make it right for you to follow this path. As believers, God holds us to a higher standard — a standard of permanency in marriage. Therefore, it is important for you to examine how you view marriage and why you believe what you do. There are Christians who assume that one Christian marrying another Christian will *automatically* mean that their marriage will be a "Christian marriage." This is not necessarily so; a Christian marriage can only be born out of the couple's determination to continually place Him at the center of their individual lives and thus in the center of their marriage. Let's look at where your beliefs on marriage may have come from and what you can do to have God's perspective.

Culture

Your parent's marriage, good or bad, has helped build your beliefs about marriage. Another major area of influence is your culture. We live in a self-centered culture steeped in entitlement. Our culture tells us that if we are not happy in our marriage, we deserve to be, and therefore it is time to get a divorce and look for someone who will make us happy.

You need to know that because you have lived in this culture (or any other culture) since birth it has undoubtedly affected your thinking concerning many things, marriage included. The sad reality is that most of the time we do not even realize the tremendous impact ungodly culture has had on us. It has seeped in by osmosis.

When we were saved, our spirits came alive and took up residence in His kingdom culture for the very first time. Yet, sadly, we entered *His* culture with the sin baggage and ungodly perspectives from our *former* culture. To live a healthy, godly lifestyle we must get rid of the old sin baggage and allow Him to shift us and give us His view.

What has your life experience and your culture taught you about marriage? It is important to your future marriage that you stop now and examine your heart. Do you have the culture's view, or God's? Whichever you hold, it will determine your beliefs toward the permanency of your marriage. You do not want to enter into marriage with a wrong perspective, because it is guaranteed to impact the health of your marriage.

Expectations

I would be remiss if I did not mention a pitfall of our culture's wrong, self-centered perspective: unrealistic expectations of our spouse. Dear ones, be alert to this! James 3:2 gives us a good dose of reality: *"For we all stumble in many ways"* (ESV). In other words, because of our sin nature, *"stumbling" is a realistic expectation in marriage!* Of course this verse is not a license to sin or be lazy, but rather it is a reminder to us of *how very much we need to rely on the Lord* in everything.

If we allow it to be, marriage can be a wonderful staging ground for godly character to be built. When I choose to lean into God, it causes me to grow. Therefore, recognizing my weakness and my husband's, I cannot expect or demand of Mike what only God can give me. Unrealistic expectations of our spouse will hurt them and our marriage. We must determine, again and again, to rely on the only One who is completely perfect. Partner with God to create a bulwark in your marriage — a bulwark that will provide protection against the onslaughts of your flesh and the enemy. How? In your weakness choose to *lean in* to Him as if the life of your marriage depends upon it — because it does. When challenges come, He alone will enable you to withstand the temptation to call it quits.

The Challenges

First Peter 4:12 warns us, *"Beloved, do not think it strange concerning the fiery trial which is to try you, as though some strange thing happened to you."* You will have times when you feel like you are in the midst of a fiery trial in your marriage. When these times come, be encouraged that this is not strange. Rather, fiery trials are actually an opportunity to allow the fire to purify us. God's design for marriage is that it would make us more like Himself; therefore, fire is necessary. If both of you are willing to embrace the fire, what an amazing difference it can make in you and in your marriage!

"Count it all joy when you fall into various trials, knowing that the testing of your faith produces patience. But let patience have its perfect work, that you may be perfect and complete, lacking nothing" (James 1:2–4). If we allow patience to have its perfect work in our hearts, the Lord will use these trials to make us "perfect and complete, lacking nothing." A fruit of this choice will be experiencing

the joy of greater freedom from our carnal nature and a greater likeness to His. When we allow the Holy Spirit to do this work in us the culture can scream "it's time to jump ship" all it wants, but hearts surrendered to Him will find that they are patiently resting in Him in the midst of the storm.

Transformation

Our carnal nature, defined another way is: "It's all about me!" We are self-centered by nature and the day-to-day interactions of marriage can provoke this nature at every turn. If things are not working the way we think they should — if we are not happy in our marriage — our carnal nature will be looking for a way out of the marriage. The reality is that rather than changing our marital status, what really needs to change is us! The fact of the matter is that we need transformation!

Romans 12:2: *"Do not conform any longer to the pattern of this world, but be transformed by the renewing of your mind. Then you will be able to test and approve what God's will is—his good, pleasing and perfect will"* (NIV). This verse is clear: we are only able to know what His "good, pleasing and perfect will" is as we submit ourselves to His renewing process for our minds. It is through this process that we learn His will for our life and marriage. Our carnal nature cries out for its own way, and this process is so challenging, especially in marriage! Yet, believe me, it is worth it!

We need a renewing of our mind in most, if not every, area of our life. It is not just about a renewal of our minds concerning the permanence of marriage; it is a renewal of any part of our minds that need to be surrendered to the Lord. His intent is that we would be in this process in an ongoing way. As you prepare to enter marriage, give yourself over wholeheartedly to the Holy Spirit's work in your life. Allow Him access to places in your heart where perhaps He has been unwelcome to go before. Make room for Him to cleanse your mind of any ungodly attitudes and lies. Then allow Him to replace these lies with His truth.

I also want to mention that this renewing process may require some personal ministry, at least initially. I believe God's heart for the inner-healing process goes beyond healing for our past; it equips us with tools for our future. At every opportunity in your marriage, the enemy of our souls will throw fodder for offense your way. Heed the words of First Peter 5:8, *"Be sober, be vigilant; because your adversary the devil walks about like a roaring lion, seeking whom he may devour."*

We regularly have choices to make that will impact our heart — and thus our today and tomorrow. What kind of choices will you make—ones that build toward, or weaken, the longevity of your marriage? Will you surrender your flesh to the One who loves and only wants what is best for you? Will you resist the enemy? Meeting with the Holy Spirit on a daily basis and allowing Him to put His finger on things in your heart can lead to a freedom and joy that you did not know possible in the past.

Challenges will come to your marriage, but I encourage you, by God's grace submit your hearts to the vision of longevity or permanence. Embracing this vision will enable you to fulfill the vows you will soon take — "For better or for worse; till death do us part" — and bring glory to Him in the process.

Three: Eternal Fruit

I find the final aspect of marital vision the most provoking of all. A while ago the Lord spoke a phrase to me: *"Marriage is not eternal, but its fruit is."* My heart felt real excitement as I heard these words; it was one of those moments when something I had grasped with my mind began to move to my heart. Yet, as I considered this phrase, I also had to remind myself that fruit can be both good and bad. Personally, I want to be alert to this. How I live my life in and through my marriage today will affect the quality of my eternity.

I want to draw your attention to First Corinthians 3:15. Speaking of the day we will stand before the Lord, this verse says: *"If anyone's work which he has built on it [the foundation of Christ] endures, he will receive a reward. If anyone's work is burned, he will suffer loss; but he himself will be saved, yet so as through fire."* This is an intense reality! What you and I build on the foundation of Christ in our marriage today and tomorrow will result either in *reward* or *loss* for all eternity!

The challenges to your flesh that will be faced head-on in your marriage are part of this. Marriage truly is one of God's tools to make us holy like Himself. His desire is to prepare us to rule and reign with Him in the age to come. It is easy for us to be taken up with this life and what it holds for us. However, we should take time to consider, as much as our minds and hearts possibly can, that eternity is our destiny. As believers in the Lord Jesus Christ, you will, I will, we all will live forever in the age to come.

Today, tomorrow, and every day we are actually living our lives for eternity's sake. According to First Corinthians, how we live each day will affect our eternity. It's hard to wrap our minds around the fact that the percentage of time we spend here on earth is infinitesimal compared to the time we will spend with God in eternity. It is wisdom to give thought to such a profound truth! Therefore, it makes sense to allow eternity to impact you now. Living in the light of eternity will affect the choices that we make from day to day. You have two choices in marriage, as in all of life — you can choose to go *your way*, or you can choose to go *God's way*. You will have to make this choice many times a day. You will experience the fruit of your choices in this life, and the impact of this fruit, whether good or bad, will follow you into eternity.

Destiny. Longevity. Eternity. Single or married, every life is to be in pursuit of the internal, external, and eternal vision that sustains a vibrant life in God.

Our Prayer

Our prayer for your future marriage is first, that you each have a vibrant personal relationship with the Lord and that you grow in vision for what He has destined for your marriage; second, that you embrace the fact that marital vision is for both this life and the next; and third, that you choose to receive His grace to live out His vision for you, both individually and corporately in your marriage.

Walking out the vision that He has for you and for your marriage will cause you to grow in holiness and to experience the joy of His rewards, both now and for all eternity. We encourage you to take up the challenge! Where it is needed, pray about and listen to the Lord concerning each aspect of His vision for your life and marriage. Then, by His wisdom, grace, and strength, walk out this vision, and enjoy all that He has for you in the process!

DISCUSS TOGETHER

1. Why is vision so important to marriage?

2. Vision's Foundation: What change or transformation are you seeking for your own heart; what character traits do you desire to grow in? Do you both have vision for growth in discipleship and the fruit of the Spirit?

3. Destiny and Calling: Have you discussed your callings with each other? If you do not each feel called to the exact same area of service/ministry, do you feel that your callings are compatible? In other words, will your marriage enhance the call of God on your life, or will your calling be hindered through marriage to each other? Have you prayed about, and discussed, what you feel the Lord is calling you to together?

4. Longevity: What have you learned about navigating the trials of life as a single person, and how will you apply this in your marriage? Knowing the ways in which you stumble, are you able to accept each other as being in process?

5. Eternity: What is your eternal vision? Do you both have a vision for the age to come, ruling and reigning with Christ in eternity? How does this vision affect your practical life today?

5

God's Amazing Design

Anne

Vive la Différence!

"So God created man in His own image; in the image of God He created him; male and female He created them" (Gen. 1:27).

Did you know that you and your fiancé are far more different than you may realize? Of course, many of these differences are already obvious to you. However, others are yet to be discovered. Primary needs, gender, temperament, and your story all come together to form and shape the person you are — both positives and negatives.

We are all familiar with the saying "opposites attract," and this is no truer than in relationships. For many married couples the unfortunate reality is that the differences that attracted them to their spouse to begin with may be the very things that tend to repel them later. Human nature is such that, perhaps without even being conscious of it, we think that others should think — and act — as we do. To us, our way seems to be *the* way. If others have another way, our natural, carnal conclusion may be: "What's wrong with them?" In reality, most often the other person is not wrong at all, they just have a different perspective, a different way of doing things. These differences can be beautiful if we allow the Lord to reveal the beauty to us.

God has a plan; He created us differently on purpose! As we submit ourselves to His ways in our marriage relationship amazing things can happen. Our hope is to see you understand how wonderfully different from each other He has designed you. The Lord desires to use these differences for your good. Rather than differences being a stumbling block, His heart is that you allow them to be a catalyst to go deeper in Him and to learn to love your spouse well.

We trust that as we look at these differences more closely and you gain knowledge, the beauty of this design will become clearer to you. Our goal is to help you understand why you are the way you are and why your future mate is the way they are, in hopes of minimizing misunderstanding and increasing cooperation. Understanding these differences will go a long way toward building a strong and healthy marriage.

You are Comparable but Different

God did not make one gender better than the other, though we are designed very differently than each other. This truth can keep you in the place of confidence in who you are in God, yet, at the same time, keep you in a place of humility, a much needed ingredient for a healthy relationship.

Our equality comes from God. He says in Genesis 1:26–27, *"Let us make mankind in our image, in our likeness, so that <u>they</u> may rule . . . So God created mankind in his own image, <u>in the image of God he created them; male and female</u> he created them"* (NIV). We were both equally created in His image — not one more than the other. Genesis 2:18 states this even more clearly: *"And the LORD God said, 'It is not good that man should be alone; I will make him a helper <u>comparable</u> to him.'"*

In our marriages, our differences can work as we learn to respect each other for who God designed us to be. We have much to learn from one another and so much to gain as we are willing to *"Receive one another, just as Christ also received us, to the glory of God"* (Rom. 15:7).

What He and She Need Most

Ephesians 5 tells us what each husband and each wife need most: *"Let each one of you in particular so <u>love</u> his own wife as himself, and let the wife see that she <u>respects</u> her husband"* (v. 33).

Future wives, I realize that respect may be somewhat of a foreign word for you — and probably knowledge of what respect is supposed to look like. Our culture does not encourage the respect of men, and if you came from a home where this was not demonstrated, you will need to be a student of respect so that you may be able to meet this need in your future husband.

Future husbands, you are given additional instruction in Ephesians 5:25. This verse charges you to *"love your wives, just <u>as Christ also loved the church</u>."* In other words, your future marriage relationship is meant to be a picture of the way Christ loves His bride, the church. The institution of marriage itself has a calling — to be a testimony to the world of how Jesus loves. This is a tall order, to be sure! If we only had ourselves to rely on, it would be impossible. However, we must constantly remind ourselves that He does not expect us to walk out any part of our life in our own strength. So be encouraged. You can exchange your weakness for His strength anytime — and when you do, amazing things can happen.

You may not think so now, but future husbands, there will be times when you do not feel like loving your wife in this way. Future wives, the same is true for you. There will be times when you will not feel like respecting your husband. What are you to do when this happens? Does Ephesians 5 have an opt-out clause? If you look at the verse again you will easily find the answer. Husbands are *commanded* to love their wives, and wives are *commanded* to respect their husbands. Commands are *unconditional*.

In a relationship conflict, crying is often a woman's response to feeling unloved, and anger is often a man's response to feeling disrespected. This is a great tip for every couple to heed. Men, if she cries, perhaps you have treated her in a way she sees as unloving. Women, if he gets angry, perhaps you have treated him in a way that causes him to feel disrespected. If this is the case, humble yourself — confess it and ask for forgiveness; this process is the only way to restore your relationship.

Temperament

Our temperaments have a huge impact on our relationship. Knowing what temperament you each are can be a tremendous help in understanding each other, and it can also be lots of fun! God can use this understanding to help you to accept one another for who you are. Acceptance is a major key to a great marriage. (We will talk more about this later.)

When Mike and I were courting, I would notice positive qualities he had that I did not possess. I really found myself feeling left out. I was pretty insecure in those days, and I would ask myself, "Why don't I think like that? Why don't I do things the way he does them?" Mike understood the temperaments and wisely gave me a book to read. By reading it I understood that I am very different from Mike. He and I have totally different temperaments, and it was God who wired us this way! It may sound silly, but it was such a relief to me to know that there was not anything wrong with me. I felt free to be who God had created me to be.

There are generally four basic temperaments. Each person tends to be a blend of two of them. Actually, the word *temperament* comes from the Latin word *temperamentum* and means "right blending." Today there are a number of tests that label temperaments with animal names, letters, or other titles. Hippocrates, a famous physician of ancient Greece, used the following terms, which are generally understood:

Sanguine — outgoing / fun loving

Choleric — leader / take-charge person

Melancholic — thinker / analyzer

Phlegmatic — easy-going

Each of these temperaments comes with their own sets of strengths and weaknesses. Knowing these encourages us in the positive qualities our temperament possesses. It also helps us to recognize our weaknesses so that we can be alert to allowing the Holy Spirit to work in these areas. We won't take the time to go into the temperaments in detail, but we suggest choosing a personality test that will help you determine which blending you are and reviewing the results together with your premarriage counselor.

One of the wonderful aspects of temperament is that, because opposites do attract, we can actually "temper" each other. Your strength will be a help to your mate in his or her weakness and vice versa; you can actually find yourselves balancing each other out. I love this aspect of temperament. Mike and I have found that we can actually enjoy each other's differences and find them even humorous at times. Our different temperaments are an opportunity for joy to flow between us — if we allow the Lord to help us accept and validate those differences.

Biological Gender Differences

As I have studied the differences between genders and how they relate to marriage I have become fascinated. I more clearly see the truth of Psalm 139:14, *"I will praise You, for I am fearfully and wonderfully made; marvelous are Your works, and that my soul knows very well."* Before we begin looking at specific brain differences between genders, it's important to understand that every person is a unique creation. During development in the womb certain hormone activity will influence the future behavior of the baby. For instance, male babies receive more testosterone than female babies. This difference will cause boys to interact differently with their environment and in their relationships than girls do.[1] There are times when a girl baby may receive more testosterone than most baby girls. This is referred to as a "bridge brain" female.[2] (There are both males and females who are considered bridge brain.)

In *Sacred Influence*, Gary Thomas explains: "Our tendency toward masculine or feminine brains occurs on a continuum, resulting in various degrees of stamping. *But, even here, a 'bridge brain' male will have more testosterone than a 'bridge brain' female"*[3] (emphasis added). In our gender-confused culture we must remember that God *is never confused* about the gender of the one He is creating; *"male and female He created them"* (Gen. 1:27).

We must be careful not to expect certain behaviors, nor be surprised by unexpected behaviors, based on gender stereotypes. Our part is to grow to know our spouse just as they are and accept them for who God has made them. It is highly beneficial to study some of the specific biological differences between men and women. These affect how we interact in marriage, and understanding them will help you respond more empathetically to your future spouse. There are actually many ways that the male and female brains differ. We will look at just a few.

Empathizers and Systemizers

"The female brain is predominantly hard-wired for empathy. The male brain is predominantly hard-wired for understanding and building systems."[4] I have noticed this in Mike and my relationship. In certain situations in the past that aroused my deep empathy, I thought that Mike was just not being very caring. Now, recognizing that he is wired differently than me has made a big difference in how my heart responds to him in these situations. Mike, on the other hand, has had to learn to be patient with me when I have difficulty understanding something on the technical side like computer functions, even when he has already told me once or twice. I need repetition because it does not come naturally to me. Understanding this difference and remembering that I am not wired the way he is has been a help.

Emotions: Staying Calm and Bonding

Generally, a female brain possesses more serotonin than the male brain. Because serotonin exerts a calming effect, a man may be prone to act in an explosive and uncontrolled manner. According to Michael Gurian, author of *What Could He be Thinking? How a Man's Mind Really Works*, "Oxytocin is part of what biologists call the 'tend and befriend' instinct, often contrasted with the 'fight or flight' instinct. The higher the oxytocin levels, the less aggressive the person is likely to be."[5] While women are generally more empathetic and less aggressive than men, it's important to note that woundedness may make someone aggressive regardless of their gender.

It is God's design that females receive more oxytocin because, by and large, in parenting it is the mother who gives the primary care to her children. The more oxytocin a female receives the greater the strength of her natural sense of bonding, and thus her desire to love and care for her children is strong. This is something that dads take time to develop. However, due to a dad's oxytocin level being lower than the mom's, dad will not experience this sense of bonding at the same level mom does. Mike's and my children are all grown adults. However, I discovered long ago that this did not change my feelings of bonding — and desire to do anything I can to help them. Mike also desires to help each one of our children in any way he can, yet he has confirmed that my desires are much stronger than his. It's all about oxytocin!

Mental Rest

I have noticed something else in my husband that is another way God has designed male and female differently. Mike has a need to take times of what Michael Gurian calls *"mental naps."*[6] Mike also likes sleeping naps as well, but

I am not referring to these. Yes, we all need to rest our brains, however, most men experience a greater need in this area.[7]

My dear lady, please pay attention! This is probably why you may find your future mate inclined to, what we might term, "veg out." Without understanding this, you may think that he is just being lazy. (Laziness is another matter altogether, and certainly a red flag in any relationship.) Even at the end of the day you are better able to process more complex entertainment due to the 15 percent more blood flow to women's brains.[8] However, his brain is tired and needs to rest. What does this mental nap look like? It may manifest in him desiring to watch a movie or television program that you do not find particularly stimulating, or he may want to spend some time alone refraining from conversation. Being a woman, you may find this a challenge, but it is definitely worth waiting for a time when he is rested and better able to hear what you are saying.

Complex Emotions

Another difference that may lead to marital conflict is the difference in each of your ability to *process complex emotional information.* Compared to women, this process may take a man seven hours longer. The scientific reason for this is that, physiologically speaking, he has a smaller hippocampus in the limbic system[9]. (The limbic system processes emotional experiences.) Females also have more neural pathways to and from this area of the brain than men do. Finally, in a man, the bundle of nerves that connects the right and left parts of the brain is about 25 percent smaller. These pathways are what enable us to process and speak with emotion.[10] This is most probably the reason he may not give you an immediate answer on something that requires emotional processing — allow him the time he needs.

Soon-to-be bride, here is a possible scenario . . . You have experienced some conflict with your husband, and you want to resolve it quickly. Honestly though, he needs time — it may take him hours to know where he stands emotionally on the issue. It is not necessarily true that a man is avoiding a discussion; he may just need to wait until he has time to process it.

I wish I had known this when we were first married. I had times of definitely misunderstanding Mike in this area. Let me share from our story. When we were courting we chose a verse that we felt would be an important foundation for our marriage relationship, Ephesians 4:26. *"Be angry and do not sin; do not let the sun go down on your anger"* (ESV). This definitely is a wonderful verse for marriage — as long as you understand what it is really exhorting us to do!

Early in our marriage if we would have a disagreement at bedtime, we would lie in bed and discuss it for a bit. I wanted to resolve it before we went to sleep, however; the next thing I knew, Mike was sleeping! I remember thinking, "How could you be so insensitive?" Then I would lie awake irritated at him. Before long I would get up and leave the room because my being irritated kept *me* from sleeping!

It took time but eventually I began to understand what the Holy Spirit was saying. He showed me that it was I who was sinning with my anger. I needed to allow Him to deal with my heart, and then I needed to *repent* so my heart could be in the place to "not let the sun go down on" my anger. It had nothing to do with Mike and I settling an issue between us before bed. *Mike was not being insensitive to me at all!* I was the insensitive one. I was demanding that he stay awake and talk things out with me. It was late and he was tired, and he needed time to process the issue before it could be settled between us.

Multitasking

Men's brains have the ability to compartmentalize while women's brains do not. Let's look at this a bit because it will be vitality important in your marriage to understand the difference between the two of you in this regard.

According to Walt and Barb Larimore, authors of *His Brain, Her Brain*, "Drs. Ruben and Raquel Gur have used functional MRIs to show that women's brains light up in more areas and use more brain pathways than men's brains when given a variety of tasks." They explain, "Because a woman's brain is so highly interconnected when compared to a man's more compartmentalized brain, women are better designed to multitask. Not only is a woman's brain designed to multitask; it virtually never turns off."[11]

"The brains of women seem to be well 'networked,' while the brains of men are much more 'compartmentalized.'"[12] This phenomenon is vividly captured in the word picture evoked by the title of Bill and Pam Farrel's book, *Men Are Like Waffles—Women Are Like Spaghetti*. Neither of these brain capabilities are superior to the other. Rather, when recognized, they can be an asset in growing to love one another, as you understand that God has designed you these very different ways for His purposes.

What might this look like in your marriage? When women speak they tend to go from one subject to the other without much clarification in between. This can make it challenging for our husbands to follow what we are saying. Our conversation can be like that plate of spaghetti . . . all mixed up together. Women experiencing a certain emotion may not be ready to quickly move out of that emotion when it's time to move on to another activity or conversation. A man, on the other hand, generally has the ability to leave something and move on to the next activity or conversation without carrying with him the influence of what he just "left." In other words, he can readily move on to something else, whereas a woman cannot do this as well.

As you can see, God has designed us wonderfully different. It takes time in a marriage to adjust to each other. Do not become discouraged, but ask the Lord for help. Our prayer for you both is that you will be willing to become a student of your soon-to-be spouse and learn how to love them just as they are. Humility — recognizing that we also have areas of our life that may be a challenge to our spouse — can go a long way toward learning how to love and accept one another.

Your Story

The last difference I want to mention is an obvious one: the differences in each of your stories, your life experiences. The family you grew up in, your birth order, how you were raised, and all the other things you experienced since birth — the good and the not so good — have helped to shape you.

God has given to each of you different gifts and has been developing these gifts in the course of your life story. They may be spiritual, physical, intellectual, or emotional. Your gifts will be a blessing and may even complement your spouse's gifts. A very practical one comes to mind for our marriage. I have never been great at math; Mike was a math major in college. I am so blessed and thankful for this because Mike handles the budget, and does a great job of it.

We bring both positive and negative things into our marriage. The positive will, of course, be a blessing to our spouse. It may be surprising to you, but the negative we bring to the marriage can also be a blessing to our spouse. How can that be? As we allow the Lord to change us, He can use our growth process to also help spiritually shape our spouse.

Let's face it, due to the culture that we live in, we all have wounds of one degree or another. Many today carry deep pain that limits their relationship with God and greatly hinders their relationship with others. Then there are those who are mainly healthy, yet still have parts of their heart that the Lord wants to touch and heal. Do not be surprised when wounds that have not yet surfaced in your dating and courting relationship arise in your married life. You can count on this because when you live together you will find yourselves triggering each other in these yet unhealed areas.

Both Mike and I came into our marriage with wounds from our past and have each received restoration in our hearts through inner-healing ministry. We cannot stress it enough — get as much healing for your heart as possible prior to marriage. We also continue to press into the Lord for His help to keep our hearts free from offense on a day-to-day basis. In marriage this is a MUST!

God loves you so much and has so much for you. Yet, if you allow hindrances to remain in your heart, you will be unable to walk in the fullness He has for you. Whenever the Holy Spirit speaks to you about something in your heart, surrender and allow Him in to bring transformation. I know that we have already said this, but it bears repeating: humbling yourself, confessing your shortcomings to one another, and forgiving each other are major keys to a wonderful and godly marriage. Without these, your marriage cannot be one that brings glory to God nor will it bring peace, joy, and life to you.

You each bring your relationship with the Lord into your marriage. You also bring the work that He has already done in your heart. You are journey mates and will be helping each other on your spiritual journey. *"He who has begun a good work in you will complete it"* (Phil. 1:6), and your spouse will be an important participant in this process.

Receiving One Another

We have different primary needs, different biological makeups, different temperaments, and different stories. Having knowledge of these can make a huge difference in the quality of your marriage. With God's help you can grow to a place of appreciating these differences — recognizing the fruit that can result in your life by responding to them rightly. Our prayer for you is that one day you will be able to say wholeheartedly that you are thankful for the differences in your spouse because the Lord uses these to make you more like Him.

Enjoy each other in your differences! It can be refreshing to discover how your spouse thinks and responds very differently than you do. You will find many differences that are definitely of a positive nature — you can gain from each other's strengths. Always be mindful that the Lord has a plan — even in the areas you find difficult to deal with in your spouse. It is not about your spouse's weaknesses but about how YOU respond. God is out to change the both of you; give the Holy Spirit the freedom to work in your heart, and allow *Him* to do the work in your spouse. This will result in much fruit in your relationship with the Lord and with your spouse.

I love the ways of the Lord! He leads two very different people to join their lives together in marriage and then amazes us at the wisdom of His design. If we are open, He can cause these differences to be complementary and instructional. I love that my husband is very even keeled; he does not get flustered easily. I, on the other hand, can be just the opposite. How thankful I am for this trait in my husband! The Lord has given me a picture of His peace and stability in Mike. I am learning more about how the Lord desires me to respond in challenges, and I continue to learn even after thirty-four years.

God's instruction for blending our beautiful, sometimes dismaying, differences is summed up in Romans 15:5–7. *"Now may the God of patience and comfort grant you to be like-minded toward one another, according to Christ Jesus, that you may with one mind and one mouth glorify the God and Father of our Lord Jesus Christ. Therefore receive one another, just as Christ also received us, to the glory of God."*

As you choose to walk out this lifestyle of being "like-minded toward one another," and to "receive one another" *in the midst of differences*, the result will be a marriage that brings glory to the God you love and serve.

REVIEW TOGETHER

Personality Profile. We highly recommend a personality profile of some kind. The couple facilitating your premarital counseling will most likely have a suggestion along these lines. If not, then you may purchase our favorite, *Wired That Way Personality Profile: An Easy-to-Use Questionnaire for Helping People Discover Their God-Given Personality*, by Marita and Florence Littauer. It sells for a few dollars — a worthwhile investment. You will each need a copy.

Appendix B, Couples Connecting. Please review Appendix B together, "Couples Connecting."

DISCUSS TOGETHER

1. In what four ways does this chapter say you and your future spouse are different?

2. According to Ephesians 5, what does HE need most? What does SHE need most? Are you committed to being a student of your spouse and discovering how you can best meet this need?

3. Have you taken a personality profile and shared the results with one another?

4. What struck you most concerning your biological gender differences? Discuss these with each other.

Notes

1   Gary Thomas, *Sacred Influence* (Grand Rapids: Zondervan, 2006), 102.
2   Ibid., 103.
3   Ibid., 103.
4   Simon Baron-Cohen, *The Essential Difference* (New York: Basic Books, 2003), 1.
5   Michael Gurien, *What Could He Be Thinking? How a Man's Mind Really Works* (New York: St. Martin's Griffin, 2004), 10.
6   Ibid., 13.
7   Thomas, *Sacred Influence*, 104.
8   Ibid., 86.
9   Ibid., 105.
10   Ibid.
11   Walt Larimore, MD and Barb Larimore, *His Brain, Her Brain* (Grand Rapids: Zondervan, 2008), 54.
12   Ibid., 54.

6

Husband and Wife Roles and Needs

Mike

Understanding personality, gender, and life histories is a monumental pillar in a marriage relationship, as Anne so aptly shared in the previous chapter. Given our very unique designs, it makes sense that each of us also have unique needs and roles within a marriage. Anne touched briefly on the immensely meaningful Ephesians 5:33, which lays out the most visible difference: men are to *love* their wives, and wives are to *respect* their husbands. Let's begin our study of these insightful instructions by extracting some other principles from this, perhaps the most prominent and oft quoted of New Testament passages on marriage. We'll first look at the beginning of Ephesians 5, where we find outlined the roles that all believers are called to fill.

v. 1. Be imitators of God.

v. 8. Live as children of light.

v. 10. Find out what pleases the Lord.

v. 17. Understand what the Lord's will is.

v. 18. Be filled with the Spirit.

v. 19. Speak to one another with psalms, hymns, and spiritual songs.

v. 19. Make music in your heart to the Lord.

v. 20. Always give thanks to God.

v. 21. Submit to one another out of reverence for Christ.

Every believer, male and female, is to pursue a lifestyle that emanates these actions. This is the fruit that is God's will for every person. Every believer is to be submitted to Christ as Lord — under His authority, in both a general and specific sense. Out of our submission to Him, we are instructed in verse 21 to submit to each other. Submitting to others includes recognizing each person's assignment in life and doing what we can to support them. Obviously limited by time and space, this will vary in proportion depending on the closeness of our relationship with the other. In a marriage the roles and needs of each partner as they follow this command intertwine in a unique dynamic that mirrors the roles of Jesus and His bride, the church. Having laid the foundation of mutual submission, the apostle Paul proceeds to specifically address the roles of husband and wife. Here it is in a nutshell:

> *Wives, submit yourselves to your own husbands as you do to the Lord. For the husband is the head of the wife as Christ is the head of the church . . . As the church submits to Christ, so also wives should submit to their husbands in everything . . . The wife must respect her husband.* (Eph. 5:22–24,33 NIV)

> *Husbands, love your wives, just as Christ loved the church and gave himself up for her . . . Husbands ought to love their wives as their own bodies . . . Each one of you also must love his wife as he loves himself.* (Eph. 5:25,28,33 NIV)

While respect and love are in every person's needs bucket, they are uniquely vital within marriage — respect and honor for the man, love and security for the woman. Though referenced in the previous chapter, it bears repeating. A man needs unconditional respect; a woman needs unconditional love.

As you ponder these roles you might agree that it's a tall order, indeed. No couple can do this in their own strength. It's a two-way street of sacrificial love. You began your relationship as friends, as brother and sister in Christ. This does not stop when you are dating or after you are married. The key is to not demand your spouse fill his or her role, but to encourage them as a friend. Submitting to one another out of reverence for Christ is what Christian friends do, and that includes the friend you will be married to. Let's clarify this point by looking at a paraphrase of Ephesians 5:22–24.

> *Wives, understand and support your husbands in ways that show your support for Christ. The husband provides leadership to his wife the way Christ does to his church, not by domineering but by cherishing. So just as the church submits to Christ as he exercises such leadership, wives should likewise submit to their husbands.* (THE MESSAGE)

A wife who has known and loved Jesus Christ as a single woman, learning to live under His leadership, can decide by the grace of God to transfer that same posture to the imperfect Christ figure of a man she will soon call husband.

Each spouse is to unconditionally love and respect the other. This is what propels us to new heights of agape love. My wife is not always easy to love nor am I always easy to respect. Our imperfections put up hurdles — that set the stage for our spouse to soar! After all, everyone has prayed at one time or another to build more spiritual muscle, right? Husbands take note of this one: *"Husbands, go all out in your love for your wives, exactly as Christ did for the church — a love marked by giving, not getting"* (Eph. 5:25 THE MESSAGE).

A husband who has known and loved Jesus Christ as a single man will have stepped into positions of leadership and service. He will also have learned about what it is to be a man, to fight and contend for justice. This will transfer as a secure covering for his bride.

As we learned in the previous chapter, it is crucial that we seek to understand our differences, including the different roles we play in the marriage. One of the greatest assets in a marriage will be the trait of humility — each spouse going low versus being demanding.

Headship and Submission

We began by looking at an outline of the actions that every believer is called to live out, then progressed to the more focused injunctions God shares that are specific to husbands and wives. Every person, single or married, is included in a strategic circle of responsibility and calling. Even when there is a clear delineation of husband/wife roles, no one is "off the hook," so to speak. In other words, no one has an easy job or some sort of advantage over the other. I like these concise definitions from author and pastor John Piper:

> Headship is the divine calling of a husband to take primary responsibility for Christlike, servant leadership, protection, and provision in the home . . . Submission is the divine calling of a wife to honor and affirm her husband's leadership and help carry it through according to her gifts.[1]

Piper goes on to say that "protection and provision both have a physical and a spiritual meaning." As a husband I need to labor and earn a living to provide things like food and shelter. I also need to provide spiritual guidance and encouragement for my wife and family. In like manner protection is in the physical realm (from an intruder or natural disaster) and in the spiritual (prayer, guarding against unhealthy influences).

A word of caution, men: we don't have to be the sole providers, but I believe we need to be primary. A minority of reverse situations does exist, where dad is a stay-at-home parent. This factor comes more into play as children are added to the family. As my wife shared in the previous chapter, women are equipped by gender (oxytocin, balanced brain function) to more effectively nurture the family on a day-to-day basis. This is not an exemption for dads by any means, simply a matter of gifting. You may have heard the common story of the mom who goes away for a weekend, leaving dad in charge of the home and two children. When she returns he tells her that he has a new appreciation for the full-time job she has! Mutual appreciation is a quality that will support and undergird our marriages.

We have encountered much in the realm of marriage conflict where the wife is frustrated because the husband is not leading, and the husband is frustrated because the wife is not following. If I had to give an unofficial estimate of which is more prevalent, I would say it's the husband's lack of providing the loving leadership his wife wants to follow. Husbands often hide their lack of leadership behind the shield of "women are to submit," forgetting they have to be going someplace in order for anyone to follow. The primary focus of each spouse ought to be fulfilling their own role, not ensuring their partner is fulfilling hers or his.

Being the "head" of the house is to be the servant of all. Husbands are clearly the Christ figure; we are called to die, to sacrifice, to lay down our lives in service to wife and family. Along with the protection, provision, and spiritual guidance mentioned earlier, I would like to add the concept of being the "point man." I love watching World War II movies, and have often seen in the script the unit advancing forward and the officer in command assigning one of his men to "walk point." This soldier would be the first to take hostile fire. This metaphor inspires me to do the same for my wife and family. I see it as a key ingredient and component of headship.

As a more mature husband, sixty-one at this writing, I have an appreciation for the long-term perspective. I'm still walking point in a way, but I am drawn to the Biblical term *patriarch*. In my opinion every husband should aspire to be an elder, not necessarily in the official position in a church, but in maturation unto becoming examples to the next generation of husbands.

Let's take a moment to clarify some of the misunderstandings that occur around these topics.

What Headship Is Not

- Headship does not give a husband unrestricted power to act on his own without consulting his wife.

- Headship does not give a husband an excuse to withhold his heart from his beloved, to be emotionally detached.

- Headship does not give a husband exemption from leadership in the home (i.e., "I've worked all day; now that I'm home I need to relax, so don't involve me in any family responsibilities.").

- Headship does not end; the journey is ongoing for as long as one is married.

As we noted earlier in this chapter, it is every believer's calling to "submit to one another out of reverence for Christ." I like this paraphrase: "Out of respect for Christ, be courteously reverent to one another" (Eph. 5:21 THE MESSAGE). Paul's admonition in Romans is comparable: "*...not to think of himself more highly than he ought to think, but to think soberly, as God has dealt to each one a measure of faith. For as we have many members in one body, but all the members do not have the same function, so we, being many, are one body in Christ, and individually members of one another*" (12:3-5). **Delusions of superiority must be ousted that we might enter into the unity to which we are called.** This is a truth for the body of Christ and essentially imperative in a marriage. Guys, be "courteously reverent" to your wife, honor her gifting and function, walk in humility, and there are likely to be no problems with submission! Gals, ditto for you on the above, and he will be more likely to grow in his leadership.

In Peter's epistle we are given clear instruction on wives submitting to husbands:

Wives, in the same way submit yourselves to your own husbands so that, if any of them do not believe the word, they may be won over without words by the behavior of their wives, when they see the purity and reverence of your lives. Your beauty should not come from outward adornment, such as elaborate hairstyles and the wearing of gold jewelry or fine clothes. Rather, it should be that of your inner self, the unfading beauty of a gentle and quiet spirit, which is of great worth in God's sight. For this is the way the holy women of the past who put their hope in God used to adorn themselves. They submitted themselves to their own husbands, like Sarah, who obeyed Abraham and called him her lord. You are her daughters if you do what is right and do not give way to fear. (1 Pet. 3:1-6 NIV)

Let's touch on the salient points in this passage. A husband who needs to be "won over" to Christ may be an unbeliever (the common interpretation here) or perhaps even a believing husband who is struggling in his faith. A submissive wife, in this case, would not chide her husband but rather exude a transforming influence. The Message paraphrase of verse one says that the husband "will be captivated by your life of holy beauty." I can personally attest to this. When my wife "submits" to me in this fashion, I get convicted and am drawn to Christ.

The "unfading beauty of a gentle and quiet spirit" is greatly appreciated by husbands. Of course, we appreciate the outward beauty as well. However, I have met many gorgeous women over the years whose lack of inner radiance all but canceled out the outward adornment. Notice how Peter states that the godly women in the past made themselves beautiful inwardly, but he also adds the phrase, "who put their hope in God." This is a trait of a submissive wife: she puts her principal hope in the promises of God, not her husband. Wives who are overly dependent on their husbands will in the end exasperate them as leaders. My wife's pursuit of and trust in God has made her an easy woman to live with. Submitting and surrendering to God is what I most want her to do.

Along these same lines, the wife who does not "give way to fear" is a blessing to her husband, especially when going through a difficult season. She will send the message to her husband in both word and demeanor that she is by his side and believing that God will come through. I must also mention here that Sarah calling Abraham "lord" or "master" was not uncommon terminology in the ancient world. My wife has come up with various endearing titles for me over the years by which she demonstrates her confidence in me. Personally, I would not want "lord" or "master" to be among them.

What Submission Is Not

Take a look at this insightful list of what submission is not, from John Piper's *This Momentary Marriage*.[2]

- "Submission does not mean agreeing with everything your husband says."

- "Submission does not mean leaving your brain or your will at the wedding altar."

- "Submission does not mean avoiding every effort to change a husband." (Best friends are honest with each other.)

- "Submission does not mean putting the will of the husband before the will of Christ."

- "Submission does not mean that a wife gets her personal, spiritual strength primarily through her husband."

DISCUSS TOGETHER

(Read the following: Ephesians 5:22–33, Colossians 3:18–19, 1 Peter 3:1–7.)

1. What does it mean for a husband to love and cherish his wife, as Christ loves the church?
2. What does it mean to live with your wife in an understanding way?
3. What does it mean for a wife to submit to her husband?
4. In what ways is a wife to show respect to her husband?
5. Should a husband or wife try to impose their personal convictions on their mate?

Ten Basic Emotional Needs

Our primary needs are to be met in Christ. One of my own sayings is, "God is **the** well from which I drink. My spouse is **a** well." To reverse the two is akin to relational idolatry. Nonetheless, we need to ascertain and gratify the needs of our spouse to the best of our ability.

Needs and roles are a wonderful complement to one another, oftentimes filling the same space, acting as a sort of two-fold cord. As I prayerfully seek to fulfill my husband role as the Christ figure in our marriage, to nurture and care for my wife, I will intrinsically be more attentive to her needs. Conversely, when I seek to meet one of her needs, say for conversation, I will be compelled to listen in the same manner that God listens to all of us, and hence motivated to fill my role.

As my wife seeks to fill her role of coming alongside me in an attitude of respect and honor, she will naturally be poised to more easily discern what I am in need of. Conversely, when she is intentional to meet my need, say for sexual fulfillment, it communicates to me that she is esteeming me as her husband. A felt need for dignity and honor is fulfilled in me. Roles and needs are many times indistinguishable.

The following list of ten basic emotional needs is adapted from Willard F. Harley's *His Needs, Her Needs: Building an Affair-Proof Marriage.*[3] Numbers are not everything, but this author has been married now for forty-seven years. There are over a million copies of his book in print, and in my opinion, *His Needs, Her Needs* is one of the best bridge building tools for a marriage. After you read over this list you will be asked to identify which needs more distinctly apply to you. Some will overlap with your future spouse and others will be unique to you.

1. AFFECTION: expressing love through words, through physical touch such as holding hands, hugs, and kisses, through notes and cards, and by creating an environment that is conducive to tender and warm feelings. This is primarily non-sexual and can be expressed any time of day.

2. SEXUAL FULFILLMENT: lovemaking, intimacy, sexual enjoyment of one another on a regular basis. Frequency is important here.

3. CONVERSATION: engaging in enjoyable topics of conversation, and talking about the events of the day, which includes how you feel about them. *Conversation* blended with *Affection* creates bonding and unity.

4. RECREATIONAL COMPANIONSHIP: doing fun things together, learning about what your partner enjoys and participating if possible, and discovering what you mutually enjoy.

5. HONESTY and OPENNESS: sharing your feelings (telling about your day, your ups and downs), initiating with your spouse ("Let's talk", asking questions), praying with one another, giving full attention (avoiding grunting responses, turning away from media distractions). This trait blends well with *Conversation*.

6. ATTRACTIVENESS OF SPOUSE: remaining physically fit and caring for one's personal appearance.

7. FINANCIAL SUPPORT: providing family finances for an acceptable standard of living, and balancing travel and work hours at healthy levels.

8. DOMESTIC SUPPORT: creating a home environment that is a refuge from the pressures of life; managing the home (including children) in a way that results in peace and order; maintaining a system for cooking, laundry, cleaning, etc.

9. FAMILY COMMITMENT: scheduling time and energy to pour into the family (both spouse and children), edifying one another, training children, going on family outings, and partnering and planning with your spouse.

10. RESPECT/ADMIRATION/HONOR: feeling value and appreciation, validation. Speak highly of your spouse in front

of others. Don't correct them in front of the children. Keep commitments. Encourage your spouse to dream, like you did when you were courting.

DISCUSS TOGETHER

1. Read over the list of Ten Basic Emotional Needs, and choose what you think will be your top five needs in marriage.

2. Rank the five you chose in the order of importance.

3. Compare them to what your future partner chose.

Notes

1 John Piper, *This Momentary Marriage*, (Wheaton: Crossway Books, 2009), 80.
2 Ibid., 99-101.
3 Willard F. Harley, Jr., *His Needs, Her Needs*, (Grand Rapids: Fleming H. Revell, 1986).

PART THREE

Conflict, Cash, and Sex

7

Resolving Conflict

Mike

Growth Through Adversity

"Behold, You desire truth in the inner being; make me therefore to know wis-dom in my inmost heart" (Ps. 51:6 AMP). The extravagance of God ensures that our growth in character will be ongoing. He *desires* that we be whole. Single or married, going deeper in being an authentic witness and display of God's grace is our life's goal. I coined a phrase years ago, "Plateaus are dangerous." When God has done a deep work in me, I may feel as if that kind of wraps things up for that sector of my life. In reality, a finished work, bearing good fruit, becomes the foundation for the next level — it doesn't indicate there is no need for further growth.

I believe that everyone who has walked with Christ has discovered that *adversity serves as a sort of depth gauge.* Pressing circumstances, or people, have a way of surfacing the things in our inmost heart that are hindering our deeper maturity. We are prone to desire an end to adversity so that we might move forward in serving God in peace. But God strategically uses adversity to move us forward in serving Him *while* we draw from His sustaining peace on the way.

Thomas à Kempis wisely observed in *The Imitation of Christ*, "How great each one's virtue is best appears by occasions of adversity; for occasions do not make a man frail, but show what he is."[1] As I pondered this, a thought came to mind: *marriage is revelatory.*

We've all visited that "count it all joy" passage in James, haven't we? Similar to other poignant Bible verses, it gives a reason for the testing process. *"Let perseverance finish its work so that you may be mature and complete, not lacking anything"* (Jas. 1:4 NIV). The fact that I've said marriage is revelatory does not necessarily indicate that I've had a turbulent marital life. The process of uniting two fallen human beings in marriage will definitely generate adversity, but marriage conflict above ground can be minimized if you will deal with issues of the heart, the things that are under the surface. *Develop a Jacob-like wrestle on the inside for truth in your innermost. It will save you many a skirmish with your spouse. Trust me.*

I recall a recent moment, not a solitary occurrence, when I emerged from a private time of prayer in the bedroom or office, feeling strong and anchored. Traveling the thirty feet or so to the kitchen, I encountered my wife. She opened a kitchen cabinet, getting in the way of what I was about to do at the counter. Imagine such a transgression! I was surprised at how a little speed bump (irritant) could so quickly surface an undesirable response from within my heart, so soon after my emerging from that wonderful time in His presence.

Every spouse will occasionally stumble in such encounters as the one described above. We need to repent, as often as needed, forgive one another and move on. It's all a part of walking in the light. Authors Gary and Betsy Ricucci insightfully observe, "One of the best wedding gifts God gave you was a full-length mirror called your spouse. Had there been a card attached, it would have said, 'Here's to helping you discover what you're really like!'"[2]

Having established adversity as a productive companion on our life's journey, we need to appropriate healthy tools by which to harness its transforming power. Let's look at several models of communication and conflict resolution that will aid us in this process.

Options in Conflict

The first model we'll use is adapted from Bob and Jan Horner's *Resolving Conflict in Marriage*.[3] They present four choices followed by three steps.

Model 1 — Choices and Steps

Four Choices in Conflict

Fight to Win: "I win, you lose. / I'm right, you're wrong." This is one person trying to dominate the other. It's the need to triumph. If you've never been trained in how to handle hurt and anger, this will be a common response to someone who does not concur with your ideas.

Withdraw: "Conflict is uncomfortable, so I need to get out of the process." If we view conflict as having no potential to be fruitful, then we will develop a hopeless attitude. Couples who believe this will end up building separate interests to avoid having to spend too much time together. Less time spent together equals less potential conflict. However, transparency and honesty will diminish.

Yield: "Fine, whatever you want is fine. It's better than arguing!" In this scenario, a safe feeling is more important to one spouse than building a close relationship. Yielding may diffuse the immediate conflict, but it opens the door to harboring bitterness. The other spouse will then be tempted to take advantage of the passive one. This only defers the conflict, it doesn't solve it, and is a major blowup waiting to happen down the road.

Lovingly Confront: "I love you and care enough about you to work on resolving the issues." This approach prioritizes the marriage relationship as of a higher value than winning, being comfortable, or escaping.

Loving confrontation is clearly the best option for a fruitful relationship, not only in marriage but also in the whole spectrum of our friendships.

Three Steps to Loving Confrontation[4]

Look Inward: Galatians 6:1 instructs us, *"Brothers, if anyone is caught in any transgression, you who are spiritual should restore him in a spirit of gentleness. Keep watch on yourself, lest you too be tempted"* (ESV). Here are the prerequisites we need to meet prior to addressing the weakness of another: be spiritual, have a spirit of gentleness, and make sure you're not tempted in the same way. Before I confront, I need to check myself to be sure I'm not moving forward in the wrong spirit, in a prideful way.

Pick the Right Time and Place: *"A word fitly spoken is like apples of gold in a setting of silver"* (Prov. 25:11 ESV). Discernment goes a long way when picking the right time and place to lovingly confront. Also, depending on how long you've been in the relationship, you will have a measure of historical insight. Remember how it went last time. What have you learned? Rehearse in your mind what your approach is going to be. What will be the best setting? What do you need to do beforehand? Perhaps send a note or a special gift? Sometimes one or both spouses need more time to process before discussing an area of conflict in depth. In that case, simply ask one another if more preparation time is needed.

Speak the Truth in Love: "*Rather, speaking the truth in love, we are to grow up in every way into him who is the head, into Christ*" (Eph. 4:15 ESV). "*Let each of you look not only to his own interests, but also to the interests of others*" (Phil. 2:4 ESV). Present the truth gently, regarding your spouse's needs as more important than your own. Truth without love inflicts injury. Love without truth robs the person of a chance to grow. I need to hear truth that I might embrace an opportunity to change and grow, but it is essential that it be presented with love.

Model 2 — Communication and Forgiveness

I was inspired when reading *Love After Marriage*, by Barry and Lori Byrne, to compile this next brief model.[5] Resolving conflict will require communication; to truly achieve this I must be willing to forgive. Resolving conflict will also require forgiveness; to truly achieve this I must learn how to communicate.

Communication Guidelines:

1. Listen closely to one another when sharing.

2. Ask questions to clarify and gain greater understanding. Here are some examples of questions to ask:

    - "I didn't understand that; could you please say it again?"

    - "Can you give me more information?"

    - "How did you feel when that happened?"

3. When your spouse is done speaking and asks you for feedback, begin with affirmation first (i.e. what you can agree with). Don't start off by defending yourself. You can share opposing thoughts

later. When you are responding to your spouse, keep in mind how you can build them up and encourage their heart.

4. Respect the vulnerability and openness with which your spouse shared. Keep it confidential. Don't use the information as leverage to support your own views or to repeat negatively in a future conversation.

Steps of Forgiving

The goal of loving confrontation is to *reconcile*, to bring *peace*. After effectively communicating, taking the next step of giving and receiving forgiveness is essential. Forgiveness is a process, and when practiced on a regular basis, it will help to minimize repeat offenses. It is perfectly normal to have to resolve issues more than once. Over time, as our hearts soften and we learn what hurts and blesses our spouse, the recovery time is shorter and the offense should occur less frequently.

Sample steps of forgiveness:

1. "Having heard your heart, I understand the painful feelings you described." Or, "Wow, now I know how I hurt you."

2. "I want you to know that I intend to work on this issue. I sincerely do want to change, before the Lord and in our relationship."

3. "Would you please forgive me?"

4. At this point it's very important that the one who was wounded says the words, "I forgive you." There is power in that declaration.

Note: if you apply these principles of listening and forgiving to the best of your ability and things don't improve, you may need third-party mediation. You may have individual issues, not related to your spouse's behavior, that need healing first.

Model 3 — The Enemy is Not Your Spouse

This final model is adapted from one of my favorite author couples, John and Stasi Eldredge, in their marriage book *Love and War*.[6]

There are times when marital conflict seems to take on a presence of its own. You get the feeling there's somebody else in the room because, in fact, there is. The same enemy that attacked you when you were single is still out to destroy you. The assault now comes on the marital front, in addition to the personal front.

Irritations are normal in marriage, right? They appear every now and then, especially when you're tired or have had a bad day at work or with the children. Stop and think of one or two irritations that are not deal breakers, but they trip you up — little speed bumps. Here is an example from the Eldredge's book. I have paraphrased for brevity.

A husband is running late, trying to head out of the house, and he's not in the mood for conversation. His wife is asking him questions as he's moving toward the door. He tries to give brief answers and displays clear body language that he needs to go. She keeps talking, and as he heads out the door and drives away, he hears the tape in his head. "She's nagging me. I hate when she does that."

The enemy now pours gas on the flames to make it worse than it really is. He gives suggestions that appear as an inner prompting. "She's always nagging you." (She's always nagging me.) "It's always been like this." (It's always been like this.) "It's never going to change." (It's never going to change.)

Left unchecked, this agreement with the accuser will result in a tiny hairline crack in the relationship's foundation. Thoughts that I allow to infiltrate will result in opinions I come to hold. We all know the danger that lies ahead.

I'll give another example from our own marriage. We were about to depart for our weekly date night one Wednesday evening. I was ready to go, but I heard Anne jogging on the mini trampoline downstairs, so I grabbed a book and read as I waited for her to finish. I was not irritated or upset at all. She came upstairs and asked if I was ready to go, to which I respond yes, and that I was just waiting for her. Her response: "I saw you shaving earlier, so I thought I would do my exercise while I waited for you." My interpretation: she was establishing the fact that she was waiting for me, not me waiting for her! Then I was irritated. She went downstairs while I walked back to the bedroom to grab my car keys, mumbling to myself something like, "You've always got to be right don't you, Anne? You're never wrong." I instantly knew that I was forming an agreement with accusation and needed to break it off. As we were backing out of the driveway in silence, I knew we had to "police the area," so to speak, and take authority over this matter. Within two or three minutes we talked it through, apologized to each other, and went on to have a nice date night!

So, let's talk about *agreements*. An agreement with accusation is allowing a negative thought or suggestion into your mind, and then allowing it to influence you. In reality, the father of lies, Satan, is deceiving us into believing something about our spouse that results in our being divided. Being the father of lies and accuser of the brethren, Satan is an expert at putting a spin on any situation. Key words to beware of are *always* and *never*. These should tip you off that the accuser is speaking. His goal is that "we believe the spin, we go with the feeling, and we accept as reality the deception he is presenting."[7]

The enemy's goal is to redefine your marriage. "The kingdom teeters on the hundred small choices we make every day."[8] The solution is very simple — ask Jesus. "Lord, what are the agreements with accusation I have been making about my marriage or towards my spouse?" Consider these examples,[9] compiled by John and Stasi, of thoughts we are tempted to agree with:

"It's just not going to get any better."
"Don't rock the boat; settle for what you've got."
"It's not worth the effort; don't give it one more try."
"Never let anyone hurt you again."
"I'm just not going to trust him/her again."
"You do your thing and I'll do mine."
"I'd be happier with someone else."

Walking out of false agreements, in both the personal and marital arenas, requires that we be "watchmen on the wall." We are responsible for what gets through the mind gate, what declarations we allow to become imbedded in our belief system. When intruders are identified, it is then a matter of making the deliberate choice for truth and reconciling with anyone we may have offended.

Here is a useful prayer outline for breaking your agreement with lies about your spouse, yourself, and your marriage. I use this tool, from *Love and War*, on a regular basis in my personal life and in my marital life; it really works.

"Jesus, forgive me for giving place to this in my heart. I reject this agreement. I renounce it. I break agreement with _____ (fill in the blank, what is it?)."

"I break this agreement and I ask for your light and I ask for your love to come into these very places. Shine your light here. Bring me back to what is true. Bring your love into this place, Lord. In Jesus' name I pray. Amen."[10]

DISCUSS TOGETHER

1. What patterns do you see in your own conflict-resolution style? Do you feel fairly proficient at it?

2. Have you been successful thus far, in your engagement, in handling conflict?

3. Do you remember how your parents handled conflict?

4. Would you agree that adversity serves as a sort of depth gauge?

5. Has your relationship thus far been revelatory — bringing issues to the surface?

6. Have you noticed any unhealthy agreements with accusations or lies?

Notes
1   Thomas à Kempis, *The Imitation of Christ* (New York: Benziger Brothers, 1895), 53.
2   As quoted in *Sacred Marriage* by Gary Thomas (Grand Rapids: Zondervan 2000), 89.
3   Bob and Jan Horner, *Resolving Conflict in Your Marriage: Leaders' Guide* (Little Rock: Family Life, 1991), 71.
4   Ibid., 75-76.
5   Barry and Lori Byrne, *Love After Marriage: A Journey into Deeper Spiritual, Emotional and Physical Oneness* (Ventura: Regal, 2012), 116-120, 132-133.
6   John and Stasi Eldredge, *Love and War: Finding the Marriage You've Dreamed Of* (New York: Doubleday, 2009), 90–97.
7   Eldredge, 95.
8   Ibid., 95.
9   Ibid., 97.
10   Ibid., 97.

8

The Healing Journey

Mike

Living together will reveal the strategic importance of the foundational structure of the heart. It is God's intent and design to strengthen your root system, to go deeper in your heart, and marriage is one primary vehicle that He uses. While dating and courtship is refreshing and light, marriage is testing and weighty. Thus every marriage will need to mine the depths of compassion, drawing from the empathy of Christ, that we might encourage our spouse in the healing process. *Husbands and wives coming alongside one another's journey of healing is a mark of authenticity in marriage.*

I said in the last chapter, "marriage conflict above ground can be minimized if you will deal with issues of the heart, the things that are under the surface." In varying degrees we all have unresolved issues from our past, painful imprints from childhood, wounds that have yet to experience a full, redemptive healing. What action should I take when I sense something coming to the surface of my heart, or in my spouse, that is affecting the peace in our marriage? How do I get in touch with these emotions and process them?

Let's first establish what our ultimate goal is. I like the trio of components put forth in *The Life Model*:

People have a God-given, inner desire to increase their maturity so they will be able to live from their hearts. Maturity is often blocked however, and the blocks usually come from absences in the other two areas – from *unfinished trauma recovery*, and from the lack of *life-giving relationships*.[1]

Over years of marriage counseling, we have observed that while the source of conflict may look like rebellion on the surface, the real culprit is mainly immaturity. That is to say, the solution to resolving marital conflict is more than just modifying behavior. Every marriage is on the way to developing a skill set and competency that finds strength and longevity via personal maturation. It's sad to see a marriage that has existed for many years but that has never matured. Here is a brief glance at the integral parts of maturity.

Maturity includes having a healthy awareness of who you are as well as taking responsibility for your own actions and feelings. **Recovery** involves acknowledging and facing our dysfunction. Getting in touch with your pain is the beginning of redeeming your pain. This is one aspect of being rooted and grounded. We're not called to live in the wound, but to live in the promise. Thus to recover we must know where the wound was formerly attached and instead apply the promise. **Belonging** is accessed from the life-giving relationships we have established.

Aside from your spouse, the cast and characters in your story will vary with the seasons. If you've been blessed with a life-long best friend then you know what belonging is — it's what you feel when you're together. Aside from the person who you're engaged to, having a core group of trusted friends is a valuable asset. Recovery and belonging cannot subsist in a relational vacuum. My wife and I have each had our own best friends over the years, and we also have couples that we relate to. Sometimes Anne will really click with the wife but the interaction between the husband and me is kind of average, or vice versa. It's rare to find another couple where both wives and husbands feel a closeness. Cherish those connections; we need to find belonging within the community of the saints, in order for maturity to blossom.

I have been a Christian for forty years and married for thirty-four. I consider myself and my marriage to be mature. By God's grace the efficacy of His promises has enabled me to conquer the pain and dysfunction from my past. Though our marriage is strong and not threatened by core conflicts, we still have a "skirmish" every now and then. Be assured that this is normal. The premise of this chapter is not that maturity will eliminate all conflict in marriage, but that healing the heart will reduce overall relational conflicts. After all, when you think about it, *burying a wound to escape its pain is actually making a place for the struggle to be kept alive within you.* So, on to a few major areas that I hope will serve as useful guideposts for your growth in maturity.

Express Your Needs

Expressing our needs is, for some of us, rather like swimming upstream. Our natural inclination is to not express needs. Most of us were not raised in a nurturing environment where we were encouraged to express our hearts. We may not have been blessed in our formative years with a loving dad and mom asking us to sit and share with them. And so we learn how to stuff things and find other means of coping and meeting our needs. Thus *most people suffer from not being heard.*

The deep down needs that we have are truly a gift of pain. They create the ache that causes us to search. This doesn't always feel good, but if we allow God to go deep the end result will be worth it. *"Counsel in the heart of man is like deep water, but a man of understanding will draw it out"* (Prov. 20:5). Husband and wife: be the person of understanding who will draw out from your spouse what he or she needs to express and understand. Christian couples are called to this. Each of your lives is hidden with Christ in God (Colossians 3:3) and in Christ are hidden all the treasures of wisdom and knowledge (2:3). I'll bet you didn't know you partnered with such a rich person! The adventure of your marriage will be a lifetime of searching out and unpacking the treasure. By natural sight the treasure is that man or woman to whom you pledged your life; by spiritual sight it's that Man, Jesus, to whom you both pledged your lives. The latter pledge fuels the former.

"God unveils his beauty to the hungry heart. His hiding of the deep things is for our protection and humility. The process of unveiling creates ownership on our part and rehabs our damaged emotions in the process . . . The divine treasure chest is unlocked as we seek and search. When I'm filled to overflowing my marriage gets the spillover. *The more beautiful God looks to me, the more beautiful my wife looks to me.*"[2]

It's virtually impossible for a married couple to grow stagnant in their relationship when each spouse is having fresh encounters with God. The joy of discovery becomes a source of strength to the marital bond. *The more I discover the treasure in Christ the more I have to invest in my marriage.*

While every couple should be this kind of resource to one another, there may be times when you will need to get counsel from a source outside of the marriage. Your spouse may not always be the most objective nor have the necessary skill set to help you process your heart in every stage. It might be as simple as meeting with a good friend to talk things out or something more formal, as in going for counseling.

Heal from Unjust Suffering

We all know the phrase, "hurt people hurt people." Nowhere is this more true than in a marriage, though our spouse is the last person we would ever want to hurt. God desires healing and its resulting freedom for all of us, but it's even more essential to pursue personal healing when the well being of another person is also at stake.

"By his wounds you have been healed" (1 Pet. 2:24 ESV). Peter is talking about suffering and endurance; his entire epistle aimed at helping us to navigate through trial and fire. His main point is that we be empowered to endure unjust suffering. Our example, he says, is Christ who suffered for us, leaving us an example to follow in His steps. Though we normally apply verse 24 to physical healing (which is okay to do, by the way) the main points in context are:

- Healing from unjust pain we've endured, whether current or past

- Healing from the sinful ways in which we've reacted to the unjust pain

Couples that actively forgive will find this healing road easier to travel. We need to release those who have wounded us and repent from the sinful ways in which we reacted to the wounding. I can distinctly remember taking years to forgive a particular person. I did it in layers, over time. When I thought I was done I would see the person or hear about them and I would still have negative feelings. My wife was a good encourager in this season, along with holding me accountable.

Taking the yoke of Jesus upon you involves this exchange. *By His wounds I am healed of my wounds.* I no longer need to bear their weight or believe their lies. The manner in which you were wounded, how you interpreted it, and the emotional implant that was left — all were borne on the cross by your Redeemer. You now have the mind of Christ available to you to replace the lies you believe about yourself with the truth of what Jesus says.

It's always a joy when I have men ask me how they can be free emotionally in order to relate to their wives on a deeper level. Such was the case with Nick. He and his wife reached a place where the joy was eroding from the marriage. He carried a lot of sadness and felt disconnected at times from his family. Whenever I hear this, I immediately think about possible times of "disconnect" in a person's past. After all, walls exist for a reason: to keep things in, or to keep things out, or both.

Over our times of praying together, Nick made some profound statements that reflected his heart condition. "Vulnerability freaks me out," was one of those statements. His parents had divorced when he was a young boy, the painful situation being more complicated when his mom remarried a short time later with no indication given to Nick until the new stepdad moved in. (If this was me, I would have erected some walls and put a crocodile moat around them!) Counseling arranged by his mom only made things worse. He was bearing a weight of suffering beyond his ability to manage.

A few weeks after we prayed, Nick had a dream. He met his pastor in a parking lot. In the dream, his pastor asked him if he would adopt an orphan. Nick asked who it was, and his pastor said, "You." The dream was a confirmation that he needed to address the pain in his childhood and allow the Lord to release healing. He did and the result was a deeper connection with his wife. Self-protection gave way to increased vulnerability.

As you prepare for marriage, take the steps needed to heal your heart. Your future spouse will be glad you did!

Beware of Transference

Transference means to convey information or content from one person, place, or situation to another. It is when I experience a person in the present as if he or she were a person in my past. It's the repetition of an old relationship — shifting of attitudes and feelings onto the new person. Pastors and leaders are especially prone to become objects of transference, as are motherly and fatherly types of people, regardless of age. Transference is a close cousin to projection.

(The unjust suffering mentioned above is a dangerous launching pad to take out our frustration on whoever might be around when we are set off. The transfer is generally towards those who are closest to us.)

Emotions can be tricky to discern. If I am experiencing feelings from the past and am able to view them objectively, then I can deal with them as feelings from the past. Otherwise we will always believe "those people out there" are the issue. The result is a further hardening of our heart and, in essence, we are fighting against the Redeemer who is intent on uncovering our issues so that He can heal them. The tragedy of this scenario is that many are living reruns of their childhood; there are different actors on the surface but the same stage, same script, and same emotions. Unfortunately, the spouse generally plays a leading role and is the prime suspect for many "emotional crimes."

Unresolved heart issues will usually turn outward in an accusatory posture. The overload of emotions in my heart seeks out a target — it may be a person, a group of people, or an organization. For example, whenever a married couple seeking counsel spends most of the time talking about the things their spouse is doing wrong, it's a sure sign that they're being affected by much more than the actions of their partner. I need to take care of my own issues, especially if there's a backlog of unfinished scripts playing out. *Radical change in my heart brings radical shift in my marriage.*

In year four of our marriage we had three children. I found myself one day experiencing jealousy over the time and affection my wife was pouring into them, especially the boys. From a rational viewpoint, I knew that I was not in any way being neglected; but since when do emotions always follow a rational route, right? I prayed into this situation, and this is what I discerned. I was raised pretty much as an only child; I had Mom's attention whenever I wanted it. But I was also starving for affection from both Mom and Dad. In my memory, I cannot recall their spending much time interacting with me on a personal level. When I realized what was generating the feelings of jealousy toward my sons, I thanked Abba for the triggers that nudged my heart to seek Him. I also confessed what I was feeling to my wife, just to make sure I had no dark corners left in this process. Further forgiveness was released to my parents, and in the end, the "child within me," so to speak, no longer saw my sons as competition.

I don't recommend trying to trace every emotional event back to some childhood root cause. We are disciples, not detectives. Renewing the mind needs to be a daily practice, and taking thoughts captive to the obedience of Christ (2 Cor. 10:5) should settle most battles. However, the saboteur of past pain must not be allowed to roam my emotions. God will help us to keep a healthy balance in this regard as He oversees our healing journey.

In year twelve our marriage was shaken due to a major career transition I was going through. I had been on staff as an assistant pastor in my first home church; all in all spending eighteen years there. Our three children, ages eight, ten, and eleven, were integrated into the church family and none of us anticipated a change on the horizon. Our pastor asked us to consider taking the reins of a small church in a nearby city that needed a new pastor. He felt it was time for me to spread my wings and branch out. The subsequent struggle in my heart was intense. Unbeknownst to me, the lack of nurture from my biological father throughout childhood was skewing my interpretation of events. These are some of the lies I was hearing: "My spiritual father is rejecting me. He doesn't care about me. He is sending me away. I must not be valuable." I was going it alone, again, just like I had to do in my formative years as a young boy. Some of what I experienced then, I was feeling once again in this season. My wife, who is my best friend, was a great support in the transition. We both agreed that I should get another perspective, and so I went to see a Christian counselor, who just happened to be an art therapist. So there I was, at thirty-nine years old, cutting out pictures from magazines to make collages! The whole idea was to get my emotions expressed into something tangible. After six weeks of seeing her, she told me I was going through grief. The pastor of the only church I'd ever known, my father figure, was releasing me from the family. In retrospect, I can see the Lord initiating me into leadership development during this time. When it was first transpiring however, I felt hurt and wounded.

Personal conflict and struggle will be our occasional companions on the journey of life. Marriage brings the opportunity to *"bear one another's burdens, and so fulfill the law of Christ"* (Gal. 6:2). My wife's intercession and encouragement was priceless. I cannot imagine what would have happened had I "camped out" in the transference, so to speak, and chosen to remain in my old identity.

Be Alert to Memories

Our brains record every memory, storing it in the vast realm of the subconscious. Comprising over 80 percent of our brain, it acts as a huge hard drive with files and folders of our entire life history. To use another illustration, consider a cluster of grapes holding anywhere from fifty to seventy-five individual grapes. If each grape is a memory event then we would have a cluster of memories. The Holy Spirit seems to choose representative memories as an entryway to the cluster. His engagement and transformation of select memories will shift the entire grouping. Jesus selects the memories that need reinterpreting; we cannot possibly visit them all in entirety.

I can recall many a conversation where I would say something like, "You know, for some reason I was remembering things from my childhood today. I don't know why; it was just random." My wife would listen, and then she would usually ask if there was any deeper application — i.e., was it something I thought I should pray into; was there any negative emotion lingering about? If it was just a memory then I would file it in the mental scrapbook; if I saw it as holding toxins then I bathed it in prayer; if I began feeling overwhelmed, I would get help. Our spouse's insight and help is invaluable as we encounter these opportunities for healing. Your partner's view can be the most objective, their compassion the most heartfelt — truly a gift from God in our lives.

A Marriage of Integrity

"Behold you delight in truth in the inward being, and you teach me wisdom in the secret heart. Purge me with hyssop, and I shall be clean; wash me, and I shall be whiter than snow" (Ps. 51:6–7 ESV). Truth in the inner parts is better than falsehood. Wisdom in the inmost place beats confusion any day of the week. A husband and wife will find peace, wholeness, and a growing maturity if they will faithfully allow God to sift and process their hearts.

"In answer to prayers for purity God allows difficult circumstances and spiritual battles in our lives that will press the heart to reveal its hidden contents. The humility and cleanness that result are foundational to Christian maturity."[3]

Consistently praying for the purity of a healed and whole heart will be an emotional antioxidant for the health of your marriage. Integrity means to be whole and undivided. A marriage marked by humility and cleanness will set the stage for unity and enable healthy fruit to emerge over a lifetime.

DISCUSS TOGETHER

1. Think about your own individual maturity level. What has been your experience with *Recovery* and *Belonging*?

2. Have you learned how to express your needs to one another and, when necessary, to "draw it out" from each other's heart?

3. Are there any areas where you have put up walls, due to past pain, that are affecting your present relationships?

Notes
1   James G. Friesen, et al. *The Life Model* (Pasadena: Shepherd's House, 2000), 45.
2   Mike and Anne Rizzo, *Longing for Eden* (CreateSpace, 2012), 138.
3   Valerie J. McIntyre, *Sheep in Wolves' Clothing* (Grand Rapids: Baker, 1996), 111.

9

Loving God with Our Money

Mike

Why are we talking about loving God with our money in a book about getting ready for marriage? The Bible mentions money over eight hundred times, and more than half of Jesus' parables talk about money. "Money matters — it matters to us, and it matters to God. That's why the Bible has so much to say about it."[1] It also matters to our marriage.

There's nothing evil about money. It's a commodity that we all need to live by. Along with communication, money often lands near the top of the list for marital discussion. Because our souls are tied to it so deeply, it has more power to affect, destroy, or build a marriage than do many other issues. The danger lies in the craving some have for more and more financial wealth, the things they do to get it, and how they then use it. We are to master money instead of having money master us.

> *But those who desire to be rich fall into temptation and a snare, and into many foolish and harmful lusts which drown men in destruction . . . For the love of money is a root of all kinds of evil, for which some have strayed from the faith in their greediness, and pierced themselves through with many sorrows.*
> (1 Tim. 6:9–10)

How much more do you think this danger is compounded within the context of two individuals trying to meld their very different approaches to money? Not only do we have lurking desires for wealth simply because of our humanness, we have honorable reasons for wanting a bit more for our spouse's sake.

In my personal life, as both a single and now a married man, I am definitely less stressed overall when finances are healthy. Conversely, when I am worried about money I am prone to be less peaceful overall and more inclined to be irritable due to budgetary discontent. Naturally, your spouse is the first receiver of whatever it is you're overflowing with.

Money issues tempt me to doubt my proficiency as a man, leading me close to developing an angry attitude. My wife might innocently remark that she thinks her car is making a noise. As my mind races to the conclusion that a noise might cost a lot and we won't be able to afford the fix, I am tempted to react unkindly. Is this a marital issue or a financial matter? The answer is yes.

Money issues for a woman in marriage tend to originate from life history. Either she is used to a certain level of wealth and expects the same in marriage, or she came from poverty and dreams of living at a higher standard. We have counseled many couples over the years that faced these scenarios.

Though they may seem small, a couple's different approaches to money will arise so regularly in a marriage they can become a deep point of contention if not openly addressed and resolved. One recurring issue in our marriage has been our differing opinions on what quality of items to purchase. My frequent quote to Anne is, "You get what you pay for." In other words, let's spend more for something that will last longer. Our backgrounds explain the tension: she was the oldest of nine children; money was tight so they bought cheap. There were only three children in our house, and my older brothers, nine and ten years my senior, were pretty much independent and on their own while I was being brought up. My parents had more to spend, thus I became accustomed to buying better quality. I do not consider this a "victory" by any means, but my wife has come to appreciate the value of a good investment.

As we look at the Lord's way of handling money and how to love Him with what He gives to us, I recommend that each of you read with an open heart and prayerfully consider your own individual beliefs about the money that God allows you to steward. Agreeing together on the principles of stewardship that will guide the use of money in your coming union is an essential step of preparation for marriage.

Wise Stewardship

As Christians, all that we have belongs to God. Our money and possessions are like the talents our Master entrusts us with and gives us freedom to use, though they are really His. The test is in whether we will be faithful or wasteful. *"The kingdom of heaven is like a man traveling to a far country, who called his own servants and delivered his goods to them . . . After a long time the lord of those servants came and settled accounts with them"* (Mt. 25:14, 19). One day we shall give an account on our oversight of both our personal and marital resources. *"It is required in stewards that one be found faithful"* (1 Cor. 4:2).

"As believers we make a bold commitment to love God with all of our strength, *which includes our money.* Jesus called this the first and greatest of the commandments — His will for us."[2] *"And you shall love the LORD your God with all your heart, with all your soul, with all your mind and with all your strength. This is the first commandment"* (Mk. 12:30).

Our money is a noteworthy element of our financial and social strength. Similar to the way we give up some of our natural physical strength when we fast from food, when we give money to build God's kingdom, our resource base becomes weaker as we fast our financial strength. This expresses love for Jesus and others, as we trust God to use the money we give for His glory. Just like fasting food or fasting our free time in Bible devotion, giving financially is fruitful for the heart. It's challenging on the flesh, especially in the beginning, but rewarding to the inner man. Seek to work the muscle of giving as a married couple. I guarantee your marriage will be blessed.

As soon-to-be newlyweds, it is essential to establish the difference between "need" and "want." Perhaps you've already encountered this, mandated by the wedding budget. Wise money management in your marriage will require the following: denying self from purchasing what you cannot afford, keeping the standard of living balanced with the standard of giving, and learning how to find contentment in the needs while saving for the wants.

When John the Baptist began his ministry he urged those he was baptizing to "bear fruits worthy of repentance" (Lk. 3:8). When the people asked him what they should specifically do, he replied, "He who has two tunics, let him give to him who has none; and he who has food, let him do likewise" (3:11). To the tax collectors he said, "Collect no more than what is appointed for you"

(3:13). His reply to the Roman soldiers: "Do not intimidate anyone or accuse falsely, and be content with your wages" (3:14). Financial principles abound in John's discourse. I see generosity and kindness in sharing, honesty and integrity to keep greed in check, and my favorite of all — "be content." Heeding John's admonition to bear these fruits will be a great asset to the growth of your marriage, both financially and otherwise.

> *"I know what it is to be in need, and I know what it is to have plenty. I have learned the secret of being content in any and every situation, whether well fed or hungry, whether living in plenty or in want. I can do all things through him who gives me strength"* (Phil. 4:12–13 NIV).

> *"Keep your lives free from the love of money and be content with what you have, because God has said, 'Never will I leave you; never will I forsake you'"* (Heb. 13:5 NIV).

> *"But godliness with contentment is great gain. For we brought nothing into the world, and we can take nothing out of it"* (1 Tim. 6:6–7 NIV).

As mentioned earlier, we may have honorable reasons for wanting to provide more for our spouse and families; this is a good desire. However, it is always best to sift these desires through the grid of prayer and make sure our motivation is pure. Early on in our marriage (it was year five, as I recall) we had three children, and up to that point we had been content with our black and white television set. But one member of the family (that would be me) wanted to upgrade. On impulse, I just stopped on the way home one day and spent over a hundred dollars (not budgeted) on a new thirteen-inch, color, "fat screen" beauty. (You won't even see these in garage sales anymore.) End of story: we all came to appreciate and enjoy viewing our programs in living color, and my wife, though a bit surprised at first, loved me through it! (Note: this was not my usual behavior. We lived, and still maintain, a very simple lifestyle. My wife gave me grace on this occasion, along with respecting me as her husband, though we did have a serious budgetary discussion in regards to the future handling of such decisions.)

Tithes and Offerings

The Bible defines where to start the journey of giving: at 10 percent. To tithe is to trust God directly with 10 percent of our money. God gives us $100, and we give $10 back to Him. When we give 10 percent of our income to God, we discover that 90 percent with God's blessing will go further than 100 percent without God's blessing. I've had couples tell me they cannot afford to tithe. The truth is that none of us can afford **not** to tithe.

God is after our heart, and one way He has chosen to get it is by addressing our attachment to money. He wants His children free from greed and confident in the wealth and generosity of their Father in heaven, so that they are released to be generous to others. *"For where your treasure is, there your heart will be also"* (Mt. 6:21).

Giving money raises emotional dynamics that force us to wrestle with covetousness and fear of lack as we demonstrate our love for Jesus and trust in our Father's ability to provide for us. Covetousness is a serious sin that defiles the heart. *"Therefore put to death your members which are on the earth: fornication, uncleanness, passion, evil desire, and **covetousness, which is idolatry**"* (Col. 3:5, emphasis mine). *"He said to them, 'Take heed and beware of covetousness, for one's life does not consist in the abundance of the things he possesses . . . So is he who lays up treasure for himself, and is not rich toward God'"* (Luke 12:15,21). May I add, "One's marriage does not consist in the abundance of things accumulated" (paraphrase mine).

To grapple with this poison of the flesh within all of us, Jesus calls us to give our money away. This aligns our hearts to grow strong in intimacy and faith. Our faith grows as we regularly experience God as our Provider. Our confidence will be enlarged as we do our part and build a history of consistent giving.

> *"Therefore do not worry, saying, 'What shall we eat?' or 'What shall we drink?' or 'What shall we wear?' For after all these things the Gentiles seek. For your heavenly Father knows that you need all these things. But seek first the kingdom of God [follow His leadership] and His righteousness, and all these things shall be added to you."* (Mt. 6:31–33)

Great joy grows as we become aware that God's eyes are on us with pleasure when we give financially. *"When you do a charitable deed [give] . . . your Father who sees in secret will Himself reward you openly"* (Mt. 6:3–4).

The widow who gave her last two mites (one-fifth of a cent) showed more love for God than those who gave much more money but at less sacrifice. Part of this widow's reward is the honor bestowed by her story's inclusion in the Word of God. *"He saw a certain poor widow putting in two mites. So He said, 'Truly I say to you that this poor widow has put in more than all; for all these out of their abundance have put in offerings for God, but she out of her poverty put in all the livelihood that she had'"* (Lk. 21:2–4). She gave much more than 10 percent. She gave sacrificially and generously. She refutes the argument in many of us that we can't afford to tithe.

We want to make use of our wealth to gain an intimate history with God, to strengthen our understanding that He's involved with the details and is indeed our Provider. He provides in many different ways. Don't disconnect God from provision because of the way it comes. Many times it's NOT a sudden check in the mail for the exact amount you need. Sometimes it's an increase in your skill, a new work opportunity, or a promotion. "As we grow in our understanding of God and gain history with Him, we're convinced of His overwhelming generosity toward us."[3] Our Father truly is the greatest giver. What He has given to us is simply amazing and humbling; we see this as we pause to reflect upon His gracious ways. This reflection compels us into generosity and extravagance, not religious obligation. The distinction between the two is important, mentioned by Paul in Second Corinthians when he speaks of preparing ahead of time to give: *"That it may be ready as a matter of generosity and not as a grudging obligation"* (2 Cor. 9:5).

Proverbs 22:9 makes clear God's priorities: *"He who has a generous eye will be blessed for he gives of his bread to the poor"* (Prov. 22:9). There is a return, or a reward, when we give that is similar to sowing seed into the earth and reaping a crop. *"Now may He who supplies seed to the sower, and bread for food, supply and multiply the seed you have sown and increase the fruits of your righteousness"* (2 Cor. 9:10). Some fear that this principle won't apply to them, that if they tithe and give away, they will be left with too little. But Scripture makes it clear this isn't the case. *"God is able to make all grace abound toward you, that you, always having all sufficiency in all things, may have an abundance for every good work"* (2 Cor. 9:8). In fact, holding on to our wealth may backfire: *"There is one who scatters, yet increases more; and there is one who withholds more than is right, but it leads to poverty"* (Prov. 11:24).

Seed and Bread

Some of the money God has entrusted to you is "seed" to sow in the kingdom and some is "bread" to eat or to use for your personal life (see Second Corinthians 9:10, above). You and your spouse must determine what amount is for each purpose. Many have a pocket full of seeds but reap no fruit because they do not sow it. We are free to choose how far we will go with God in giving. We are all developing our approach to the area of giving financially, and the counsel of Scripture leads us toward generosity. *"He who sows sparingly will also reap sparingly, and he who sows bountifully will also reap bountifully. So let each one give as he purposes in his heart, not grudgingly"* (2 Cor. 9:6–7). Luke 6:38 expands on what it means to reap bountifully: *"Give, and it will be given to you: good measure, pressed down, shaken together, and running over . . . For with the same measure that you use, it will be measured back to you."*

As we give, we produce thanksgivings towards God and partner with Him in the storyline of blessing others. He writes this down and remembers our contribution to building His kingdom. He gives us opportunity not only to participate but also to be remembered in doing so. Cornelius, who honored God with his wealth and was generous to the poor, was given an angelic encounter, a memorial in heaven, a home visit from an apostle of Jesus, salvation for his whole house, and the filling of the Spirit — and his salvation provoked a revival in the Gentile world! *"A devout man who feared God with all his household, gave alms generously to the people, and prayed continually to God . . . 'Cornelius, your prayer has been heard and your alms have been remembered before God'"* (Acts 10:2, 31 ESV).

As a couple about to enter into marriage, where your financial decisions will be made jointly, having a solid understanding of the Bible's instructions and God's rewards for generosity, tithing, and giving is essential. Be intentional to reflect on God's provision in your life. Share about it with friends and family as a means of encouragement. Set your heart to give freely and cheerfully

(2 Cor. 9:7). Start with a prayer, "Jesus, help me to see how You give freely and cheerfully to me, so that I can do the same." Give according to what you receive (see First Corinthians 16:2). Work out what would be a tenth of your combined income and determine to put it aside for God. Commit to give systematically and prayerfully. Don't slip into a religious mode. Stay connected to God's heart every time you give. Talk to Him along the journey — remember, we're committing to love God with our money. It's about relationship not a random ritual. As you prepare for marriage, give serious thought to any needed course adjustments in your financial paradigm. Similar to other areas of spiritual growth, this will be a work in progress.

Let's consider some practical aspects of your finances. Delve a little deeper together into the details with the DISCUSS TOGETHER questions below, and then begin to form a budget using the worksheet provided in Appendix C.

DISCUSS TOGETHER

1. How are you paying for the wedding?
2. Have you grown together in making financial decisions thus far?
3. Do you share a common view on tithing?
4. Who will decide when to give extra offerings?
5. Who will be the primary money manager?
6. Will you have joint or separate checking accounts?
7. Will you maintain a monthly budget?
8. What is your philosophy on credit cards and borrowing money?
9. Do you plan to make out wills?
10. How often do you think you will go out to dinner?
11. How much cash will you both normally carry with you?
12. Were you both raised with a similar standard of living (rich, poor, middle class)?
13. What did you learn from your parents in the area of financial planning, shopping habits, and generosity?

GETTING STARTED WITH A BUDGET

1. List your individual income, expenses, and debt, using the "Household Budget" worksheet in Appendix C. (Consider making extra copies before you begin.)

2. Establish realistic goals for getting out of debt.

3. Monitor your spending. Tracking expenses, even small purchases, over a month's time can reveal places where you may need to cut back.

4. Celebrate when you reach financial goals. Work toward a reward!

Notes

1   Adapted from sermon notes by: Wes Martin, "Loving God with Our Money," Forerunner Christian Fellowship, Grandview, MO, 5/25/2014. http://www.ihopkc.org/resources/weekend-services/fcf/#

2   Ibid.

3   Ibid.

10

Sexuality in Marriage

Mike

(If possible, we suggest covering this material when the wedding is imminent.)

"God doesn't turn His eyes when a married couple goes to bed."[1] In his classic, *Sacred Marriage*, Gary Thomas delves into this almost scandalous truth, concluding that we, in turn, "shouldn't turn our eyes from God" when we ponder this subject of intimacy with our husband or wife. God created the sexual experience, and to Him, under the one-flesh marriage union, it is holy. The fact of the matter is, Anne and I pray (inwardly for the most part) before and during our sexual intimacy. It's no different than any other area of our marriage. Asking God for guidance is always recommended and beneficial.

Theology of Sex

Early Church Fathers

While we've received many wonderful blessings in our Christian heritage, we have come to discover that no one is perfect or infallible. Consider these men of God from the early centuries and their views on sex, which have influenced the church. Clement of Alexandria said that sex is only for the purpose of bringing forth children. Origen's view was that the Song of Solomon is allegory only and has no physical application. Augustine believed that sexual intercourse transmitted original sin. And then there is Ambrose, who said it was a venial sin to engage in marital relations for pleasure only.

Much of this thinking reflects a Greek rather than Hebrew philosophy. Thankfully, the Jews had a much more accurate outlook on sex. "To the ancient Jew, nothing was more important than the preservation and purity of the family line."[2] However, in Jewish culture, the purpose of sexual relations went beyond simply procreation.

Jewish View of Sexuality

Thomas tells us of a famous Jewish rabbi, Nahmanides, who was born in Spain and later lived and died in Israel. In his thirteenth-century work, *The Holy Letter*, the rabbi described physical intimacy as a type of spiritual encounter. "Through the act (of intercourse) they become partners with God in the act of creation. This is the mystery of what the sages said, 'When a man unites with his wife in holiness, the Shekinah is between them in the mystery of man and woman.'"[3]

I think that most would agree that we need to adopt a more Jewish view of sexuality. "God made flesh, and when God made flesh, he created some amazing sensations. While the male sexual organ has multiple functions, the female clitoris has just one — sexual pleasure. By design, God created a bodily organ that has no other purpose than to provide women with sexual ecstasy. This wasn't Satan's idea; it was God's. And God called every bit of his creation 'very good.'"[4]

Regardless of whether you were previously active sexually or if you are a virgin, there's no way to predict how your relationship will flow in this area once you're married. We can, however, rest in the fact that God created man and woman to be sexually compatible, and barring any physical problems, sex is almost instinctive. Unlike what the media and culture might express, you don't have to try it first to know for sure that you will be able to meet one another's sexual needs.

When we teach marriage seminars I always read the following verse: *"Let your fountain be blessed, and rejoice in the wife of your youth, a lovely deer, a graceful doe. Let her breasts fill you at all times with delight; be intoxicated [ravished] always in her love"* (Prov. 5:18–19 ESV). I make it a humorous point, just to relax everyone, but this verse rings true for most guys. I also call attention to the fact that out of more than seven billion people on the planet, my wife is the only one to whom I relate sexually. We are exclusive, and only she is to ravish me with her love.

Hindrances

There's an old saying that "Satan will do everything to get you into the bedroom before you're married, and everything he can to keep you out of the bedroom after you're married." To put it another way, he attempts to entrap us in lust, to defile us, and then in frustration, to deny us the marital pleasure that God intended.

Over our years of doing marital counseling, we've found that hindrances in the bedroom are a major source of contention for couples. Here are three common root causes.

1) *Abuse.* A young boy or girl whose sexual boundaries were violated can be left with varying degrees of impediment in the sexual realm. **Shame** – "I am defiled. I'm not worthy. So I cannot allow myself to be free or to be known." This causes a retreat into one's self. **Powerlessness** – being sexually overpowered will cause a person to be protective, and rightfully so. "How can I trust that I won't be taken advantage of again?" A sense of being **depersonalized** – "Who am I, and does my lover really love me for who I am?"

As I mentioned in chapter 8 (The Healing Journey), husbands and wives need to come alongside of each other to encourage the process of transformation that is underway in all of our lives. I have heard many tragic stories in the counseling room of young boys and girls whose personal boundaries were violated. Thankfully, I have partnered with many, as well, who have received the restorative intervention of our loving God. In the words of Psalm 30:11, *"You have turned for me my mourning into dancing; You have put off my sackcloth and clothed me with gladness."*

While acknowledging God as the One who heals the effects of sexual abuse, we recognize that along with prayer there are specialized resources available to assist men and women to heal from past sexual wounding. Books, support groups, and seminars are invaluable tools in this regard. I have listed a few titles in the Recommended Reading (Appendix G).

2) *Street Education.* Being taught by peers instead of loving and wise parents sets a person up to develop an incomplete and potentially damaging view

of sex. This can be greatly distorted, riddled with falsehoods, and extremely ungodly. Young boys are often influenced to view sex as some kind of trophy to win, falsely proving their developing manhood. Young girls are the target of Satan's enticement to find security and acceptance by offering a sacred part of their personhood, one that is reserved for expression only in godly covenant relationship. Those of us who were not raised in a Christian community of family and friends, and were subject to the immorality of the day, were left especially vulnerable to negative sexual imprinting.

In my own life, forty years of walking with Christ and thirty-four years of marriage at this writing, I am still accountable for stewardship over my sexuality and keenly aware of the enemy's desire to drag me back into my perverted origins. Depending on the uniqueness of your experience, you may be prone towards an idolatrous, self-serving sexual disposition, or perhaps you have a repugnance that drives you to self-protection. Sadly, there are married couples that have opted for abstinence as a permanent solution.

Let me be clear in stating that there *is* victory, no matter what mountain you may feel is standing in the way. I advise that you approach sexuality in marriage, and its subsequent unfolding over the years, as a *process*. Mature, married friends, pastoral advice, and a good book here and there will be reliable guideposts for the journey.

3) *Improper Home Education.* This is a sort of "adjunct" to the previous section. Parents need to make choices on how to tastefully talk about sex to their growing children. Depending on their own personal healing and comfort level on the topic, education may range from zero (the subject never came up) to an extreme negativity on the subject. In my own upbringing, I had zero on both counts. I wasn't taught, and I wasn't cautioned. This left me with my peer group, media influence, and my own imagination.

Purity and truth are a restorative balm for the soul. No matter your sexual past, the blood of Jesus cleanses from *all* sin. *"Therefore there is now no condemnation [no guilty verdict, no punishment] for those who are in Christ Jesus [who believe in Him as personal Lord and Savior]"* (Rom. 8:1 AMP). Repentance and cleansing will loosen the soil around those stubborn lies we believe. Regularly exchange any lies for God's truth. Set your heart to believe what God says about you. It will serve your marriage bed well.

Spiritual and Emotional Components

Our one-flesh union has emotional and spiritual components that must be integrated in order for the physical aspect to be fulfilling. Just to review, chapters 5 (God's Amazing Design) and 6 (Husband and Wife Roles and Needs) speak at length in regards to this. A healthy sexuality needs a good foundation to rest on. It is not a stand-alone component. In the context of marriage, *best friends will have the best sex.*

Gary Thomas nails it: "Remember that in Christian marriage, husband and wife are more than lovers. They are brother and sister in Christ."[5] This reality transcends physical pleasure. It doesn't replace it, but it transcends it. As a matter of fact, if you focus on spiritual revival in your marriage, it will keep at bay the little foxes that might threaten your sexual life.

Equally important is the consideration of our expectations. What kind of intimacy are you expecting? Here is a good rule of thumb on expectations: *keep them realistic and reachable.*

I have also developed a non-physical expectation — I expect our sexual union to produce a spiritual benefit. I most definitely enjoy the physical pleasure, but it is momentary and fleeting. The spiritual union continues on and is an important source of sustenance for the bulk of our relationship. I see it as the completion of a circuit. The relational connect (emotional and spiritual) is a support for the physical; the physical connect is a support for the relational. They co-exist in the marriage stream, and the bedroom is a part of that stream.

Especially vulnerable to unrealistic expectations are men who have come out of sexual addiction. The "tolerance effect" of addiction creates the need for new and exciting levels of stimulation. Transferred into marriage, this becomes an unfair expectation to place on a spouse, because fantasy is not reality. If sexual addiction has been present (and it's primarily a guy thing) it needs to be taken seriously. We recommend that sobriety from sexual addiction for at least six months be a requirement before a couple proceeds with marriage plans. Some premarital counselors are stricter and say one year; others more lenient, suggesting at least three months of being free.

On the female side, fantasy is often composed of a non-sexual attraction — perhaps to that special guy on your favorite television show or in that fiction series you are reading. You know, the guy who has it all together and manifests every attribute you could ever wish for in a husband. "Why can't my husband be just like him?"

The bottom line for husbands and wives: get help if you need it, and be honest with your future spouse.

Sex is the Calling to Connect

There have been a few times in our marriage when we had plans for sex and they were challenged by a disagreement during the day. This is bad timing for an argument. So there we are, naked as jaybirds, sitting in bed – **talking**. A situation like this is a great motivation for guys to resolve conflict. Ideally, we seek to grow, mature in character, and love one another out of our love for God. It's what we're commanded to do. Realistically, it doesn't hurt to have a physical need giving a little extra push in the right direction.

It's a great place to meet and "check in." Ironically, when your clothes are off it can uncover other things. Also, in the midst of a busy life, it may be the first time all day that you've had meaningful conversation.

Guys tend to get frustrated when heart issues spring up when it's time for sexual intimacy. They may feel their time is being infringed upon. Truth of the matter is: problems that manifest in the bedroom, at the worst possible time, just before sexual intimacy, would not even have come up had you not been planning sexual intimacy. In other words, sexual intimacy is so sensitive and precious that it helps to surface the things we would have just swept under the rug.

Men and women view sex very differently. Guys' view: the passion and intimacy in the bedroom make every other area of the marriage so much nicer! Girls' view: the passion and intimacy in every other area make the bedroom so much nicer! As I see it, this is one of those both/and scenarios. Sex is God's creation and very important in a marriage, but it is proportionately the servant of the whole. My own experience, along with over three decades of pastoral ministry, leads me to the estimate that approximately 2 to 4 percent of our time as a married person will be spent in the sexual realm.

Wives desire intimacy in the areas of intellect, emotion, and spirituality. These are the areas by which you came to know each other. Over time, they deepened to the point of deciding to be married. *They were, and always will be, the sure foundation to an enduring marriage.* Nonetheless, sexuality in marriage remains as that small but strategic element — invaluable to the overall health of a marriage. This has led us in our marriage to plan regularly occurring "in-home dates," as we like to call them. This has removed uncertainty and doubt, and in their place is a regular orderliness that we both appreciate. "What about being spontaneous?" you might ask. It's always a welcome guest, but we find that planning ahead of time is much more reliable. The renewal that sex has brought to our marriage over the years has inspired us to make sure we are consistent.

"Sex is perhaps the most powerful God-created way to help you give your entire self to another human being. Sex is God's appointed way," says Tim Keller, author of *The Meaning of Marriage*, "for two people to reciprocally say to one another, 'I belong completely, permanently, and exclusively to you.'"[6] Keller gives this great summary: "A covenant is necessary for sex. It creates a place of security for vulnerability and intimacy. But though a marriage covenant is necessary for sex, sex is also necessary for the maintenance of the covenant. It is your covenant renewal service."

Honor One Another

Though mentioned in a previous chapter, it bears repeating: once you are married, you should not engage in sexual behavior that causes either of you to feel pain, disrespect, or shame. Intimacy between husband and wife is a sacred gift that should never evoke feelings of guilt, shame, or disrespect. *"Honor marriage, and guard the sacredness of sexual intimacy between wife and husband"* (Heb. 13:4 THE MESSAGE). Having the physical, emotional, and spiritual well-being of the other person in mind is essential. To honor someone is to give them respect and dignity. This is how the entire body of Christ is to minister to one another. Whether the same or opposite in gender, we are the support structure for one other. *"Be devoted to one another in love. Honor one another above yourselves"* (Rom. 12:10 NIV). In the marital arena, we remain as brother and sister in Christ, but also enjoy a transcendent component of interaction.

These next two sections may or may not have much relevance at the moment. If you are both virgins going into marriage, they undoubtedly will simply be conceptual. However, I guarantee they will be useful principles for the future. If applicable, simply peruse for now and bookmark for later.

Seven Characteristics of a Creative Lover

In their excellent premarital manual, *Called Together*, Steve and Mary Prokopchak give us great marital advice for the bedroom.[7]

Be Totally Available (see First Corinthians 7:3–5). Do not deprive your husband or wife except for prayer and fasting. Schedule nights for time together. What is at stake when you say no? Feelings of rejection can develop.

Be Carefree. Know that sexual response for a woman is tied to her emotions. Put your cares aside and freely give yourself to one another. If there is a lot on your mind, pray, then give each other a back rub. If there is hurt between you, work it out before lovemaking.

Be Attractive. Appearance affects our attraction to each other. Take care of yourself (shower, shave, make-up, etc.).

Be Eager. Anticipate sexual experiences with one another. [And I will add that there will be times when you will need to display agape love on the front end. Don't worry about "faking it." Love is an action.]

Be Creative. Study your spouse. Find out what excites him or her. Pursue creative avenues to ignite these desires.

Be Interested. Do not let lovemaking become predictable and boring. Sex will lose its interest if you are not involved in doing things differently. Communicate about this.

Be Uninhibited. Accept yourself. Your spouse chose *you*. Do not get hung up on imperfections. Do the things that you can do. Come to terms with how you look. Don't compare yourself [to any other marriage, person, or to media images].

Understanding Our Differences

Shaunti and Jeff Feldhahn have teamed up to write men- and women-specific books with great practical insights. Their book *For Men Only*[8] contrasts four of our sexual differences.

One: She has a lesser motivation towards sex, which she would alter, if possible. "Men have more testosterone-type hormones linked to 'assertive' sexual desire. Women have more estrogen, which is tied to what is called 'receptive' sexual desire. Which means they tend to be available but simply don't have as much craving to pursue it."[9] This hormonal difference results in women being prone toward distractions (examples: a noise in the house, kids making noise, or leftover thoughts from the day). Meanwhile, the man is in his sex compartment and hears nothing. She is more sensitive and feels the potential hindrances to the process much more that her husband. Physical exhaustion is another roadblock. Guys, being visually stimulated, can muster up the strength even if they're tired. Women need to work harder in this regard.

Two: She needs more time to get in the mood. A guy's sexual engine is pretty much always idling. A woman needs some time. Jeff Feldhahn relates this great word picture from a wife:

> "It's not that I don't want to make love, but at the end of a long day with four kids, my mind is set on a course like a cruise ship headed for port... that quiet bit of space a mom anticipates when the kids are asleep, the chores done, and the house quiet. And just as I'm within sight of that port my hubby rolls over and says, 'Whatcha doin' over there?' It's not that I don't want to be with him, but, mentally it's like trying to stop a cruise ship that's going full steam ahead and making it turn on a dime. I can't quite turn off the day and do an about face in the blink of an eye like he can."[10]

Practically then, for us guys, we may need to slow down and give her brain a chance to catch up. Or, provide some anticipation time. I call this a "statement of romantic intention." It could be in the morning, afternoon, or early evening. Point is, you don't surprise her as her head is hitting the pillow in exhaustion.

Three: Your naked body (no matter how muscular) does not by itself turn her on sexually. Guys see an attractive woman and the dial moves on our body meter. It's automatic. Our wives are not aroused in the same way. Most women do not struggle with the lust of the eyes in the sexual realm.

Four: For her, sex begins at the heart level. "Her body's ability to respond to you sexually is tied to how she feels emotionally about you at the moment. If she's not feeling anything in her heart, her body's sex switches are all the way over on 'off' . . . She's not keeping score, by the way. She just can't help it. For her, those two things — what's in her heart about you and how she can respond sexually — meld into one."[11] This quote sums it up: "All my power to turn you on is how I look. But where you have power, and where I don't, is how you treated me today. It's all emotional."[12]

If I were viewing sexuality through the grid of painting, I would categorize it as an accent color. It's not primarily on most of the walls, but it adorns the whole in a beautiful way. It's similar to the way a woman accessorizes her outfit; jewelry and scarves, for example, just seem to tie it all together. If sex is removed from the marriage relationship, there will be an incompleteness, an adornment lacking, and a subsequent hindrance to unity left in its absence.

Dr. Louis Evans Jr., writing for the *Mastering the New Testament* commentary series, says it well: "The one flesh in marriage is not just a physical phenomenon, but a uniting of the totality of two personalities. In marriage, we are one flesh spiritually by vow, economically by sharing, logistically by adjusting time and agreeing on the disbursement of all life's resources, experientially by trudging through the dark valleys and standing victoriously on the peaks of success, and sexually by the bonding of our bodies."[13]

DISCUSS TOGETHER

1. Have you discussed each other's previous sexual experiences? (Note: be general and non-graphic.)

2. Is there anything that embarrasses you about having sex? Any apprehension?

3. Do you have realistic expectations about your honeymoon, or are you expecting a Hollywood version of lovemaking? Review the section in this chapter on "Understanding Our Differences."

4. Do you think that talking to express your preferences will ruin the romantic mood during sex? (e.g., to say "I like that," or "Please don't do that." How else will your partner know how to please you if you don't express it?)

5. Have you discussed birth control? (See Appendix A.) Who will be responsible for birth control?

6. Have you discussed your desire to have children, including how soon, how many, and how close together?

Notes

1   Gary Thomas, *Sacred Marriage* (Grand Rapids: Zondervan, 2000), 201.

2   Ibid., 205.

3   Nahmanides, *The Holy Letter* (Brooklyn: Ktav Publishing House, 1976), 60.

4   Thomas, 206.

5   Thomas, 209.

6   Timothy Keller, *The Meaning of Marriage* (New York: Dutton, 2011), 223.

7   Steve and Mary Prokopchak, *Called Together* (Camp Hill: Christian Publications, 2003), 65-67. Used by permission.

8   Shaunti and Jeff Feldhahn, *For Men Only: A Straightforward Guide to the Inner Lives of Women* (Sisters: Multnomah, 2006), 126-136.

9   Ibid., 127.

10 Ibid., 131-132.

11 Ibid.,135.

12 Ibid., 136.

13 Louis H. Evans Jr., *Hebrews: The Communicator's Commentary Series* (Waco, TX: Word Publishing, 1985), 243.

PART FOUR

Fruit That Remains

11

Marriage Within the Bridal Paradigm

Mike

There are many paradigms in Scripture that illustrate and clarify truth. Very common are the agricultural ones, which people in the agrarian society of Bible times would readily grasp. In addition, there are military and economic metaphors used in Scripture. Jesus introduced what is known as the "bridal paradigm" to the church, referring to Himself as a bridegroom in the Gospel of Matthew. *"Can the friends of the bridegroom mourn as long as the bridegroom is with them? But the days will come when the bridegroom will be taken away from them, and then they will fast"* (v. 9:15). He compared the kingdom to His Father arranging a marriage for Him (v. 22:2). In the parable of the wise and foolish virgins, He emphasized the importance of prayer (getting oil) in order to relate to Him as the Bridegroom, *"Then the kingdom of heaven shall be likened to ten virgins who took their lamps and went out to meet the bridegroom"* (v. 25:1). The bridal paradigm is meant to engage us in a greater depth of obedience to the first and greatest commandment: to love God with our whole heart, soul, mind, and strength. As we will see, this concept spans the whole of Scripture, Old Testament to New.

Bridal Portraits in the Old Testament

Hosea is the first prophet who portrays God as a husband to Israel. Hosea 2:19-20: *"I will betroth you to Me forever; Yes, I will betroth you to Me in righteousness and justice, in lovingkindness and mercy; I will betroth you to Me in faithfulness, And you shall know the Lord."* Isaiah stated: *"For your Maker is your husband, the Lord of Hosts is His name"* (54:5). Jeremiah develops the theme in Jeremiah 2:2, *"Thus says the Lord: 'I remember the devotion of your youth, your love as a bride, how you followed me in the wilderness, in a land not sown'"* (ESV).

Ezekiel is brought into the intensity of God's emotions towards Israel, and in Ezekiel chapter 16 we see a very painful allegory of unfaithful Jerusalem. The Lord was gracious to save her from her shame, spreading the border of His garment over her and making a covenant to love and care for her. In response, she chose a path of idolatry and spurned the love of God. This is a "tough read" chapter, but thankfully it ends with a promise of restoration.

Of these four prophets, Hosea and Ezekiel are bookends that contain the most personal of marital experiences, which paralleled their ministries. Hosea was asked to take a prostitute as his wife — one whom God knew would be unfaithful to the prophet. This was an invitation into the fellowship of His sufferings, for God was experiencing an unfaithful wife in the nation of Israel. God manifested an unrelenting love through His servant Hosea to illustrate how He feels toward us. Ezekiel had an even more intense experience. He received this word from God: *"Son of man, with one blow I am about to take away from you the delight of your eyes"* (Ezek. 24:16 NIV). Within twenty-four hours his wife died. That same phrase, "delight of your eyes," was also applied to the way in which Israel formerly felt toward the sanctuary where they met with God. They had strayed away again, losing the object of their affection. This was a grief to the heart of God. These two prophets experienced the intensity of brokenness, separation, and unfaithfulness.

Throughout the Scripture, God frequently uses the relationship of man and wife to illustrate humans' relationship with Him, and to expose the true states of our hearts. Geoffrey Bromiley, former professor of church history and historical theology at Fuller Theological Seminary, sums it up thusly: "Do we not learn from Israel what sorry specimens of married partners we really are? Should we not learn from God what it is to be a real partner in marriage?"[1]

Another prophet through whom God expressed His heart on marriage was Malachi. *"Judah has dealt treacherously, and an abomination has been committed in Israel and in Jerusalem, for Judah has profaned the LORD's holy institution which He loves: he has married the daughter of a foreign god"* (Mal. 2:11).

Marriage is a holy institution because God sanctified it, set it apart, to be a reflection of Jehovah and His people, Christ and His church. More than a simple metaphor, marriage is to be a living model, one that will incarnate and model the relationship that Jesus desires with every person. Great is the zeal in the heart of God to see this truth unfold, and His passion is fierce against every enemy that would contest it.

"'For the LORD *God of Israel says that He hates divorce, for it covers one's garment with violence,' says the* LORD *of hosts. 'Therefore take heed to your spirit, that you do not deal treacherously'"* (Mal. 2:16). To deal in a treacherous way is to be disloyal, unfaithful, providing insecure footing or support.[2] A good word picture would be *quicksand*. Our modern church culture of self-gratification is in dire need of receiving this stern warning against treachery, for God promises a few verses later that He will sit as a refiner:

> *"But who can endure the day of His coming? And who can stand when He appears? For He is like a refiner's fire and like launderer's soap. He will sit as a refiner and a purifier of silver; He will purify the sons of Levi, and purge them as gold and silver, that they may offer to the* LORD *an offering in righteousness"* (Mal. 3:2-3).

Within the context here, the Lord is still talking about His heart toward marriage. This incarnation of the bridal paradigm, my marriage and your marriage, will be purified and refined. It is a holy institution that must be kept holy. Jesus is zealous about this. He will be intentional in our marriages, leading us to greater depths of transformation.

In the ancient method of refining, the metal would be kept in the fire until the dross was removed. The molten hot liquid, with dross skimmed off, would eventually reflect the image of the refiner as he gazed upon it. Hence the goal of our marriages: the image of Christ being seen and reflected. As I mentioned in the last section of chapter 8, *a husband and wife will find peace, wholeness, and a growing maturity if they will faithfully allow God to sift their hearts.* This wonderful (though often difficult) process, which you have no doubt found to be strategic in your spiritual growth as a single person, will continue to be a valuable asset in your marriage journey.

Unpleasant circumstances and conflict are inevitable in life. If we come to appreciate their transformative power as tools in God's hands, we will more quickly rise above the enemy's intentions. *Dross is just as unsightly when concealed as when revealed, and being brought to the surface earmarks it for potential removal.*

Bridal Portraits in the New Testament

In the aforementioned references from the Gospel of Matthew we heard from Christ Himself on His role and calling as the Bridegroom. There are clear teachings on this subject in the New Testament.

The apostle Paul was a great spiritual father who trained up many in the faith. He made a great impact upon the people in the city of Corinth to whom he penned several letters. *"Even if you had ten thousand guardians in Christ, you do not have many fathers, for in Christ Jesus I became your father through the gospel"* (1 Cor. 4:15 NIV). Years later, when their fidelity was being undermined by false apostles, he expressed his concern: *"I am jealous for you with a godly jealousy. I promised you to one husband, to Christ, so that I might present you as a pure virgin to him. But I am afraid that just as Eve was deceived by the serpent's cunning, your minds may somehow be led astray from your sincere and pure devotion to Christ"* (2 Cor. 11:2–3 NIV).

Paul pictures himself as the father of the bride, and the jealousy he felt was the same as Father God's own jealousy for the undivided loyalty of His people. Paul was a true "friend of the bridegroom," aiming to present wise virgins, full of oil, to their Bridegroom.

A few years later, writing from prison, Paul expresses his heart once again. He first quotes from Genesis, then applies it to Christ and the church, and ultimately every marriage: *"For this reason a man will leave his father and mother and be united to his wife, and the two will become one flesh.' This is a profound mystery — but I am talking about Christ and the church. However, each one of you also must love his wife as he loves himself, and the wife must respect her husband"* (Eph. 5:31–33 NIV). Christian marriage is called to be a reflection of the union between Christ and His church. It is meant to tell the story of faithful, covenant love. It was God's intention in the garden, was perfectly modeled by Christ, and is the mandate for every marriage today.

Perhaps the most dramatic New Testament display of the bridal paradigm is in the book of Revelation. *"Let us be glad and rejoice and give Him glory, for the marriage of the Lamb has come, and His wife has made herself ready.' And to her it was granted to be arrayed in fine linen, clean and bright, for the fine linen is the righteous acts of the saints. Then he said to me, 'Write: "Blessed are those who are called to the marriage supper of the Lamb!"'"* (19:7–9).

The *Expositor's Bible Commentary* tells us, "The wedding supper began toward evening on the wedding day, lasted for many days, and was a time of great jubilation. Here in Revelation, the wedding is the beginning of the earthly kingdom of God, the bride is the church in all her purity, the invited guests are both the bride and the people who have committed themselves to Jesus."[3]

Additional bridal language follows as John's apocalyptic vision unfolds: *"One of the seven angels who had the seven bowls full of the seven last plagues came and said to me, 'Come, I will show you the bride, the wife of the Lamb.' And he carried me away in the Spirit to a mountain great and high, and showed me the Holy City, Jerusalem, coming down out of heaven from God. It shone with the glory of God, and its brilliance was like that of a very precious jewel, like a jasper, clear as crystal"* (Rev. 21:9–11 NIV). The reality behind this imagery is stunning — shrouded in mystery, yet clear enough to pursue. Married couples who fix their gaze on this glorious future culmination will find their present marriages infused with new vigor.

At the close of the book of Revelation, the return of Christ comes in the midst of the church crying out in her bridal identity: *"The Spirit and the bride say, 'Come!'"* (v. 22:17). God ends His sweeping story of redemption and hope with the promise of an ultimate wedding, and ushers us into an eternity defined by that marriage relationship. The marriage of Christ and the church is the flawless prototype (and thus, guide) for our earthly marriages, not the other way around.

DISCUSS TOGETHER

1. Do you think it would be an issue in a marriage if one spouse understood and was excited about the bridal paradigm while the other spouse was not interested?

2. How important is it to have similar theology and the same spiritual opinions? Is there room for differences?

3. Do you both embrace the concept of being refined to reflect the image of Christ?

4. What are your thoughts on the bride of Christ presented in the book of Revelation? Do you think that meditating on these passages would affect your marriage in a positive and practical way?

Notes

1 Geoffrey W. Bromiley, *God and Marriage* (Grand Rapids: Wm. B. Eerdmans, 1990), 34.

2 *Webster's New Collegiate Dictionary*, 1974, s.v. "treacherous."

3 Alan Johnson, *The Expositor's Bible Commentary: Revelation, Volume 12* (Grand Rapids: Zondervan, 1981).

12

A Fruitful Investment

Mike

Premarital counseling is one of our favorite activities. We share in the joy of each couple as they have found that special one to be their life partner. Celebration is certainly in order, as the search can be a sometimes long and exasperating process. What makes it so special for us is that we are called upon to regularly reflect on our three decades of marriage as we guide couples through the preparation process. *Every fruitful field of our married life has been the result of sowing seed,* soaked in much prayer and the utter graciousness of our God. Our goal, then, with couples on the front end of the journey, is to ready a field for sowing that will produce a harvest in the years ahead. On the surface, the wedding gets a lot of attention; it's what everyone sees. Our burden, however, is building a foundation for a life-long marriage, and a godly marriage, in turn, creates a harvest that will last with us into eternity.

Joyful harvest is often preceded by a drought, or as in the case of Israel, a time of captivity. When the Lord moved upon the heart of King Cyrus to restore the Jewish people to their home, it was like a dream come true. Captivity is a time of having little seed to sow, and hence it is precious. *"Those who go out weeping, carrying seed to sow, will return with songs of joy, carrying sheaves with them"* (Ps. 126:6 NIV). Another translation reads: *"He who goes out weeping, bearing the seed for sowing, shall come home with shouts of joy, bringing his sheaves with him"* (ESV).

This principle of "carrying seed/carrying sheaves" applies in many areas of life. *When you sow you reap.* One area that contains daily encounters in the field is the marriage relationship. Weeds and stones that were covered over or simply not noticed in the high-altitude air of courtship begin to manifest. The quick investment/quick return that seems to be the norm **before** marriage develops into selfless pouring in and then waiting **after** marriage. Long investment/long return is not nearly as fun.

There is a deep correlation between the style of our discipleship and our style of relating in marriage. Those who sow bountifully into their spiritual lives will also reap bountifully. The harvest we reap through seasons of following Christ provides the seed to sow for the next planting. The same cycle holds true in marriage. On the flip side, those who sow sparingly will reap in like fashion.

Seed bearing couples will be those who enjoy the sheaves of harvest — fruit to last an eternity.

Your Marriage in Light of Eternity

Anne

I was raised in a family that attended a church — yet we did not know the Lord. During this time in my life I would often find myself sitting alone on our front steps pondering a variety of things. (With eight siblings this was a place I could go to find quiet and be alone.) I distinctly remember that one of the subjects I mused over and over was the concept of eternity. At times I would feel almost overwhelmed with the vastness of it. I kept thinking, "It just keeps going, and going, and going."

Now being forty years in the Lord I cannot say that I understand eternity any better, but . . . I no longer find it unsettling to think about. On the contrary, it is the hope of my heart. As a matter of fact, thinking about being with the Lord in eternity often puts a smile of anticipation on my face.

How about you? Have you given much thought to eternity? If not, I encourage you to do so. Think of it — the life you live in this mortal body is less than a snap of the fingers compared to the future you have there. While discussing writing this chapter, a friend said something that I believe can help you better understand what I hope you gain from reading: "If you do not have a grasp of the dailiness of eternity, you lose the ability to lay things down."

In our chapter "Marital Vision," I shared a phrase that the Lord dropped into my heart about eternity. *Marriage is not eternal, but its fruit is.* I want to inspire you to grow godly fruit in your marriage, fruit that will follow you into eternity. On the day we stand before the Lord we will encounter both reward and loss. *"If anyone's work which he has built on it [the foundation of Christ] endures, <u>he will receive a reward</u>. If anyone's work is burned, he will suffer loss; but he himself will be saved, yet so as through fire"* (1 Cor. 3:14–15).

Jesus made it clear that eternity is something to prepare for: *"Do not lay up for yourselves treasures on earth, where moth and rust destroy and where thieves break in and steal; but lay up for yourselves treasures in heaven, where neither moth nor rust destroys and where thieves do not break in and steal"* (Mt. 6:19–20).

There are both earthly treasures (ones we are *not* supposed to lay up) as well as heavenly treasures. Earthly ones are not always tangible and seen — some are intangible and unseen. One particular earthly "treasure" has an insidious way of feeding our flesh — and this very much to the detriment of our relationship with God, others, and especially our spouse. It is the treasure of *self.*

We need to ask ourselves: am I a "driven" person motivated by my compulsion to succeed and achieve recognition? Do I look out for my own interests but very little for the interests of others? (See Philippians 2:4.) When I really think about it, do I mainly live to make things better, or more comfortable, for *me*? These are earthly treasures — treasures that those without the hope of Christ are left to resort to. These heart attitudes may seem to be helpful temporarily in this life, but they will undermine your marriage at the deepest level, and are more than counter-productive for the next.

It is clear that the Scriptures exhort us to live with eternity in mind. Ecclesiastes 3:11 tells us that *"He has put eternity in their hearts."* C.S. Lewis in his landmark *Mere Christianity*, states it well:

> If I find in myself a desire which no experience in this world can satisfy, the most probable explanation is that I was made for another world. If none of my earthly pleasures satisfy it that does not prove that the universe is a fraud. Probably earthly pleasures were never meant to satisfy it, but only to arouse it, to suggest the real thing. If that is so, I must take care, on the one hand, never to despise, or be unthankful for, these earthly blessings, and on the other, never to mistake them for the

something else of which they are only a kind of copy, or echo, or mirage. I must keep alive in myself the desire for my true country, which I shall not find till after death; I must never let it get snowed under or turned aside; I must make it the main object of life to press on to that other country and to help others do the same.[1]

The life you live in your marriage will be very much about your eternity. I want to encourage you; as you prepare all the necessary details of your wedding day, even more so prepare your heart for what lies beyond that day — a marriage for God's glory, with the ultimate destination being our "true country," as Lewis so eloquently stated. *"But now they desire a better, that is, a heavenly country. Therefore God is not ashamed to be called their God, for He has prepared a city for them"* (Heb. 11:16).

Since marriage is not eternal, but its fruit is, what should you aim for as you prepare for marriage? What could this fruit look like over future decades of married life? Galatians 5 outlines the possibilities: both the fruit of the flesh and the fruit of the Spirit. The fleshly fruit is so easy to come by, naturally. Paul says, *"The works of the flesh are evident . . . But the fruit of the Spirit is love, joy, peace, longsuffering, kindness, goodness, faithfulness, gentleness, self-control"* (5:19, 22–23). This is the kind of fruit we want to carry into eternity.

If you both give yourself to growing in God, you will bear abundant godly fruit, individually and in your marriage relationship. This is the fruit that remains — a heavenly harvest for the ages.

Notes

1   C. S. Lewis, *Mere Christianity* (New York: Harper Collins, 2001), 136-137.

13

Married in Exile

Mike

My wife and I are both citizens of another country besides the United States. Our citizenship is in heaven, and we wait for our transport there. Imagine being exiled to another country. I would have a longing that increased over time to return home. My place of origin (Buffalo, NY) and my current home (Kansas City, MO) would be beckoning me to return. If my wife shared the same passion we would be bonded on a deep level. We would "create space" for each other in the waiting. But consider if only one spouse had a yearning to return. What if one became content in exile? A major component for attachment would instead become a disconnect.

A citizen is a legally recognized member of a country or state. If you're married you may recall getting your marriage license from your local county or city. To legally dissolve it you would need the court's permission. Christian marriage adds another dimension; your marriage license is recognized in heaven. To legally dissolve it you would need heaven's permission. Our citizenship in heaven defines our individual lives, and so it should define our life together.

I won't be married to my wife in the age to come, but our expectation of eternal life is a source of strength to our marriage today. It motivates us to rise above the petty troubles that seek to sabotage our home, and to stir the power of the age to come, already a resident deposit within our hearts. We have *"tasted the good word of God and the powers of the age to come"* (Heb. 6:5). Like Abraham, we are waiting for *"the city which has foundations, whose builder and maker is God"* (Heb. 11:10). It's ironic that a strategic component of any marriage is one that transcends the life of the marriage.

A healthy marital gaze is to look beyond your spouse to see Christ. The point is to seek to minister to Jesus as you're interacting with your partner. In the end it's about Him receiving glory. Our marital agreement on this point helps to keep our marriage expectations reasonable and maintain a greater measure of diligence. As I shared in *Longing for Eden*, "We have a vital role to play in intercession and daily interaction that will have great bearing on one another's eternal rewards. The judgment seat of Christ will produce eternal rewards on our individual behalf even though we worked as a team to compile them."[1]

Waiting Together

Waiting is easier when you're not alone. Having a partner in waiting, someone to talk with, seems to make the wait more enjoyable. Biblically speaking, waiting is to gather around a promise. I like the way that Henri Nouwen describes the visit of Mary to Elizabeth — two women pregnant with very unusual promises. "By being together these two women created space for each other to wait. They affirmed for each other that something was happening that was worth waiting for."[2]

They were part of a company that also included Zechariah, Simeon, and Anna. These people were serious, hard-core waiters! The Messianic promise was delayed by centuries, hence very few were still gathering around it. I've observed a similar scenario in people who resign from their Christian faith because they're tired of waiting. Life has worn them out; what they wished for hasn't come true. Our postmodern culture has seduced their focus and drained their zeal; they have succumbed to the wayward majority. (Postmodernism in a nutshell: there are no absolute truths and we must be "tolerant" of other views.)

It's dangerous if you're waiting for something but not sure what it is you're waiting for. You would be hard pressed to find someone at the airport just waiting around without a ticket to somewhere. There has to be an absolute destination. That is, I will not tolerate flying anywhere except the location printed on my ticket.

Here is a Biblical definition of waiting, from Bob Sorge's *The Fire of Delayed Answers*: "How to wait: run after Him with all your heart, mind, soul, and strength. Waiting is aggressive repose. Waiting is a stationary pursuit. Waiting is intense stillness. Waiting is vigilant listening."[3]

As Anne clearly stated in the last chapter, we are to live with eternity in mind, waiting for Messiah's second coming and the unfolding of God's promises. Our father in the faith, Abraham, set the tone for the walk of faith we are called to. *"By faith he lived as a foreigner in the promised land, as in a strange land, living in tents [as nomads] with Isaac and Jacob, who were fellow heirs of the same promise. For he was [waiting expectantly and confidently] looking forward to the city which has foundations, [an eternal, heavenly city] whose architect and builder is God"* (Heb. 11:9–10 AMP).

What Abraham was waiting for, John saw: *"Now I saw a new heaven and a new earth, for the first heaven and the first earth had passed away . . . Then I, John, saw the holy city, New Jerusalem, coming down out of heaven from God, prepared as a bride adorned for her husband. And I heard a loud voice from heaven saying, 'Behold, the tabernacle of God is with men, and He will dwell with them, and they shall be His people. God Himself will be with them and be their God'"* (Rev. 21:1–3).

Father Abraham and the apostle John — two inspiring figures whose vision was for another time and another place, as ours should be.

As individuals and marrieds, we are caught in the crossfire between the "great cloud of witnesses" and the great crowd of this present age who have yet to find a grid for life beyond the temporal. The former inspires us to throw off what hinders, the sin that entangles, and to run the race with eyes fixed on Jesus (see Hebrews 12:1). The latter tempts us to seek eternal fulfillment from temporal sources or perhaps to follow after Jesus when it's comfortable and convenient.

The Allure of the Temporal

When temporal sources become a final "destination" of sorts, we begin to reason and make choices as if this present life is all there is. It's not long before we find that our zeal to passionately follow after God wanes. *"And because lawlessness will abound, the love of many will grow cold"* (Mt. 24:12). Lawlessness entails the casting off of restraint, the loss of vision. The result: love grows cold. When the pressures of life crash in upon us, it's time to stay focused. This holds true for every disciple, whether single or married. Jesus gives an illustration in Luke chapter 17 using as a backdrop the days of Noah and the days of Lot.

Let's consider the marriage alluded to in this chapter — Lot and his wife, exiles from Sodom.

Without going into all the particulars of the pressing circumstances in Sodom, we observe two characteristics in this marriage and family: spiritual dullness and passivity. The angels sent to rescue Lot urge his quick response to escape the city. They implore him to gather his family. His sons-in-law thought it was all a joke and did not even respond. Again, they urge Lot to gather his wife and daughters; Lot hesitates. Finally, the angels must grasp them all by the hands and pull them away.

"Flee for your lives! Don't look back, and don't stop anywhere in the plain! Flee to the mountains or you will be swept away!" (Gen. 19:17 NIV).

Once again Lot has issues and finds it too challenging to simply obey. He fears that the mountains are too far away and so asks instead if they would be permitted to flee to a small town nearby. At this point the angels acquiesce and grant amnesty to this small town, named Zoar ("little" or "small"). Remember that fear was the motivation. Later on we read that "Lot and his two daughters left Zoar and settled in the mountains, for he was afraid to stay in Zoar. He and his two daughters lived in a cave" (19:30 NIV).

Lot brought his fear to the small town — the place he thought would be safe. Compromise will always lead you to a smaller place. In the end he went to the mountains anyway, which was the first directive issued by the angels. When the Spirit is calling for urgency and my response is casual or fear-based, I'm not likely to make the right decisions. What looks safest is usually not the place of enlargement. This is a spiritual life principle; it works in marriage too.

"In that day, he who is on the housetop, and his goods are in the house, let him not come down to take them away. And likewise the one who is in the field, let him not turn back. Remember Lot's wife. Whoever seeks to save his life will lose it, and whoever loses his life will preserve it" (Lk. 17:31-33).

I think we would do well to remember something that Jesus specifically tells us to remember. What was her issue, anyway? Lot's wife wasn't just taking a glance backward; more than likely they all were. I believe that Lot's wife was going back. They were already in Zoar, a place of safety. The smoke was rising from Sodom. Who would return to such a place of destruction? A closer look at Genesis 19:26 gives insight: *"But Lot's wife looked back, and she became a pillar of salt"* (NIV). The word for "looked back" is the Hebrew *nabat*. It means: to scan, to look intently at, and to regard with pleasure or care. May I understate something? One major problem in Christian marriages is that one or both spouses have ceased moving forward. Our gaze must be on our ultimate destination together: eternity.

The word of the Lord was clear to Lot's family, and it's clear to us as well. His wife's decision affected not only her own life — the family repercussions were devastating. Disharmony in a marriage leaves gaps in the psyche of the children. Living in a cave with their father, Lot's older daughter decided that the best way to ensure that their family line continued was to have relations with him. They got him drunk and each daughter became pregnant. The result was the birthing of the Moabite and Ammonite families, which became a thorn in the side of Israel and Judah in later years.

It's impossible to know what kind of marriage Lot had, how he led his wife and daughters, and what he could have done differently that might have possibly saved his wife's life. I've seen a husband or wife make bad decisions all on their own while surrounded by good, solid family. The main lesson for us is to note the words of Jesus: "Remember Lot's wife." Singles, marrieds, families — we are not called to lawlessly cast off restraint or focus on the temporal; we are called to be *"children of God without fault in the midst of a crooked and perverse generation . . . shine as lights in the world"* (Phil. 2:15). Of necessity we must be a "forward people" and pledge our hearts like Ruth of old: *"Entreat me not to leave you, or to turn back from following after you; for wherever you go, I will go"* (Ruth 1:16). Going back is not an option.

An appropriate verse to apply here is Luke 9:62: *"No one who puts a hand to the plow and looks back is fit for service in the kingdom of God."* I once looked at this verse as kind of a qualifying factor; i.e. if you start to follow God but look back, He will disqualify you. But it really isn't about performance or being accepted. The word *fit* means "well adapted." If I'm prone to keep looking back, I won't adapt well to God's ways. So if someone isn't fit for service in the kingdom of God, it isn't because they didn't make the cut. It's more like this: hands that don't stay on the plow never till the forward ground; and when our hearts are in this condition we are not going to fit or adapt well to God's ways. Consider this paraphrase: if you put your hand to the plow and keep looking back, you will not adapt well to what I have ahead for you.

Divorce is the decision made by a spouse to take their hands off the plow. Failure to move forward becomes the enticement to look back. Singleness begins to take shape as a new destination, a chance at a fresh start, a lightening of the load. It's really a mirage of the enemy, a false transition being offered with a so-called new beginning that's actually hollow and filled with regret.

The Power of Anticipation

Have you ever known a child who is looking forward to a gift or a reward? I remember the day we announced to our three young children that we would be taking a family vacation to Walt Disney World. We set them up for a surprise, gave them a few clues, and then played a video that revealed the destination. They were eagerly waiting from that day forward! The promise was sure, and the day did indeed arrive. We all have first-hand experience in this joy of anticipation and we never grow out of the wonder of it. Looking forward to a special weekend away, a family vacation, a special date night — all serve to energize us in some way.

Earthly marriage is a season of bridal preparation (Revelation 19:7). It serves as a pointer to the most glorious wedding ever. The anticipation of the future wedding of the Lamb releases hope and joyful expectation. The gaze toward the future fuels the present.

What renews an individual? What renews two individuals living together in holy matrimony? It's the eternal glory. It's fixing our eyes on what is unseen, what is coming ahead. Timothy Keller describes it well in his book *Prodigal God*: "We are all exiles, always longing for home. We are always traveling, never arriving. The houses and families we actually inhabit are only inns along the way, but they aren't home."[4]

> *So we do not lose heart. Though our outer self is wasting away, our inner self is being renewed day by day. For this light momentary affliction is preparing for us an eternal weight of glory beyond all comparison, as we look not to the things that are seen but to the things that are unseen. For the things*

that are seen are transient, but the things that are unseen are eternal. (2 Cor. 4:16–18 ESV)

This glorious truth needs to light every marriage path, in the words of A.W. Tozer, "like an illumination from some other sun, giving us in a quick flash an assurance that we are from another world."[5]

The hour in which we live is not a time to cast off restraint or focus on the temporal; it's a time for husbands and wives to contend for fresh, eternal vision in their marriages. Your individual response and your marital response to the commands of God will transcend this life and be conferred as rewards in the age to come.

Jesus commended His disciples who left all to follow Him, promising blessing both in this life and in the "age to come" (Mk. 10:30). It is the future kingdom where we will continue to serve as kings and priests in our resurrected bodies. Jesus made the age to come an object of present experience when God became a Man, when the Word became flesh. He delivered us from this "present evil age" (Gal. 1:4). By our partaking of Christ, we taste of the powers of the age to come (Heb. 6:5). Unlike any earthly power, this is the most potent resource for our marriages.

Husbands and wives who invest in the age to come are "laying up treasure," some of which will spill over into the here and now, and solidify their marriage in this age. "Every marriage must choose its world. A marriage invested in the age to come will reap the greatest return in this age. That's the romance of the sojourning. It consists of two lives, visionary partners gathered around the promise — married in exile, longing for Eden."[6]

One of the meanings of the word *vertical* is "situated at the highest point."[7] *"God raised us up with Christ and seated us with him in the heavenly realms in Christ Jesus"* (Eph. 2:6 NIV). This is the destination of the Godward journey. It's the best place to personally abide and the best place for your marriage.

DISCUSS TOGETHER

1. As a single person, have you experienced the groaning of creation, a longing for the age to come and the fulfillment of all things?

2. How important is it to have a like-minded marriage partner who feels what you do?

3. Do you feel confident that your love will not grow cold, that you will keep your hand to the plow? What about your future spouse?

Notes

1   Mike Rizzo, *Longing for Eden* (CreateSpace, 2012), 144.

2   Henri Nouwen, *Finding My Way Home* (New York: Crossroad Publishing, 2001), 102.

3   Bob Sorge, *Fire of Delayed Answers* (Canandaigua: Oasis House, 1996), 189.

4   Timothy Keller, *Prodigal God* (New York: Dutton, 2008), 95.

5   A.W. Tozer, *The Pursuit of God* (Harrisburg: Christian Publications, 1948), 78.

6   Rizzo, 147.

7   *Webster's New Collegiate Dictionary,* 1974, s.v. "vertical".

PART FIVE

Resources

APPENDIX A

Birth Control

Family size is a very important topic for engaged couples. Do you desire to have children, and do you have control over when and how many? We encourage couples to discuss birth control with their pastor and trusted married friends, and to also read up on the subject. The following article by Matt Perman is from DesiringGod.org, the website of author and pastor John Piper, and we have found it to be an excellent resource.

Does the Bible permit birth control?[1]

Desiring God and Bethlehem Baptist Church have no formal position on birth control, but John Piper and most of the pastors on staff believe that non-abortive forms of birth control are permissible. The Bible nowhere forbids birth control, either explicitly or implicitly, and we should not add universal rules that are not in Scripture (cf. Psalm 119:1, 9 on the sufficiency of Scripture). What is important is our attitude in using it. Any attitude which fails to see that children are a good gift from the Lord is wrong: "Behold, children are a gift of the Lord; the fruit of the womb is a reward. Like arrows in the hand of a warrior, so are the children of one's youth. How blessed is the man whose quiver is full of them" (Psalm 127:3-4).

There are, of course, some Christians who would disagree with this position on birth control. Some of the major theological objections that have been made to birth control can be categorized according to the following questions:

Is birth control consistent with the truth that children are a gift from the Lord?

It is very important to delight in the reality that "children are a gift of the Lord." But some people go further and argue from this that since children are gifts from God, it is wrong to take steps to regulate the timing and number of children one has.

In response, it can be pointed out that the Scriptures also say that a wife is a gift from the Lord (Proverbs 18:22), but that doesn't mean that it is wrong to stay single (1 Corinthians 7:8). Just because something is a gift from the Lord does not mean that it is wrong to be a steward of when or whether you will come into possession of it. It is wrong to reason that since A is good and a gift from the Lord, then we must pursue as much of A as possible. God has made this a world in which tradeoffs have to be made and we cannot do everything to the fullest extent. For kingdom purposes, it might be wise not to get married. And for kingdom purposes, it might be wise to regulate the size of one's family and to regulate when the new additions to the family will likely arrive. As Wayne Grudem has said, "it is okay to place less emphasis on some good activities in order to focus on other good activities."

When I was teaching a summer course at a seminary in Africa, a student of mine made a perceptive observation along these same lines. He noted first of all that in the creation account the command to multiply is given together with the command to subdue the earth: "And God blessed them; and God said to them, 'Be fruitful and multiply, and fill the earth, and subdue it; and rule over the fish of the sea and over the birds of the sky, and over every living thing that moves on the earth (Genesis 1:28)." He then asked how a farmer (he lived in a largely agrarian society) knows how much land he should cultivate. The answer, of course, is that a farmer seeks to cultivate what he believes he can reasonably handle. He doesn't take this command to mean that he needs to make his farm be as large as is naturally possible. Likewise, then, it is right for a couple to seek to have the number of children that they believe they can reasonably nurture in light of the other callings they may also have on their lives. In the same vein, Wayne Grudem points out: "We aren't required to maximize the amount of children we have any more than we are required to subdue the earth all the time—plant, grow, harvest, etc."

In reality, then, although it is true that "blessed is the man whose quiver is full of [children]," we need to realize that God has not given everyone the same size quiver. And so birth control is a gift from God that may be used for the wise regulation of the size of one's family, as well as a means of seeking to have children at the time which seems to be wisest.

Shouldn't we let God determine the size of our family?

Sometimes people also reason that if you really want to "trust God" to determine the size of your family, then you should not use birth control. The assumption seems to be that if you "just let things happen naturally," then God is more at work than if you seek to regulate things and be a steward of when they happen. But surely this is wrong! God is just as much in control of whether you have children when you use birth control as when you don't. The hands of the almighty are not tied by birth control! A couple will have children precisely at the time God wants, whether they use birth control or not. Either way, then, God is ultimately in control of the size of one's family.

The "trust God, therefore don't use birth control" thinking is based upon the incorrect assumption that what happens "naturally" reflects "God's best" for our lives, but that what happens through human means does not.

Why should we conclude that the way to let God decide the size of our family is to get out of the way and just let nature take its course? We certainly don't think that way in other areas of life. We don't reason, for example, that we should never get haircuts so that "God can decide" the length of our hair. Farmers don't just let the wind plant their crops in the fear that actively regulating what is grown on their land somehow interferes with the provision God wants to give them. And a family doesn't just trust God to provide food by waiting for it to drop from the sky, but instead goes to the store and buys it. God ultimately determines everything that will happen, both in nature and in human decisions, and He brings His will to pass through means. Human activity does not therefore interfere with His plans, but is instead itself governed by Him as the means to bring to pass His will. Hence, we should not conclude that what happens apart from our planning is "better" and more reflective of God's desires for us than what happens through our planning. God very often causes us to plan as the means towards improving our lives and advancing His kingdom purposes.

Further, God has revealed that it is His will for us to regulate and direct creation for His glory (Genesis 1:28). God has given us the privilege of being able to make significant life decisions because this exercises wisdom and thus shows the fruit that His word is bearing in our lives. When we rightly use the godly wisdom God has given us, God is glorified. He doesn't want us to simply think we have to take what comes naturally, apart from our efforts, because then our sanctified wisdom is not expressed. In fact, very often it is God's will that we not simply let things move along naturally. Going back to the analogy mentioned above, farmers don't simply collect whatever grain happens to grow in their fields, concluding "this is what God wants to provide." Rather, they go out and plant grain, realizing that God wants to provide not only through nature, but also through the means they employ to steward nature.

It does not work, therefore, to conclude that the use of birth control interferes with God's role in granting children. Birth control can be a way of wisely stewarding the timing and size of one's family. One might be able to minister more effectively for the kingdom, for example, by waiting 3 years after marriage to have children in order to enable the husband to go to graduate school. And one might be able to minister more effectively for the kingdom by deciding to have 4 children instead of 15, so that more resources can be given to the cause of missions and more time can be devoted to other areas. If such planning is done for God's glory and in wisdom, and if such planning continues to acknowledge that our plans are not perfect and that birth control does not absolutely ensure anything, it is pleasing to God.

Does birth control express a lack of faith in God?

Without regulating the size of their family, many couples would end up having more children than they can reasonably support financially. In response, some argue that we should simply have faith that God will provide the funds. However, we don't use the "God would provide" reasoning to justify going beyond our means in other areas of life. We wouldn't consider it wise, for example, to pledge twice our annual income to missions organizations in faith that God will supply the extra funds. God expects us to make wise decisions according to what He has given us, and not presume upon Him providing from out of the blue. Reasonable financial considerations are a relevant factor: "If anyone does not provide for his own, and especially for those of his household, he has denied the faith, and is worse than an unbeliever" (1 Timothy 5:8).

Should natural family planning be preferred to "artificial" contraception?

Some conclude that "natural family planning" is acceptable but "artificial" means are not. But this seems to overlook something significant: in both cases, you are still seeking to regulate when you have children. And so if one concludes that it is wrong to seek to regulate the timing and size of a family, then it would have to be concluded that natural family planning is just as wrong as "artificial" means. But if one concludes that it is appropriate to steward the timing and size of one's family, then what makes "artificial" means wrong but natural family planning right? Surely it is not because God is "more free" to overrule our plans with natural family planning! Perhaps some have concluded that artificial forms are wrong because they allow one more fully to separate intercourse from the possibility of procreation. But if it is wrong to have intercourse without a significant possibility of procreation, then it would also be wrong to have intercourse during pregnancy or after a woman is past her childbearing years. There is no reason to conclude that natural family planning is appropriate but that "artificial" means are not.

Questions may arise about particular methods of birth control and potential abortifacient qualities. Here is an excellent synopsis from Lauren Enriquez, former legislative associate for *Texas Right to Life*.

> Some methods of family planning only prevent conception, and others prevent conception and have the potential to cause an abortion when a woman does conceive. Barrier methods (like condoms and diaphragms), fertility awareness methods (like Natural Family Planning), surgical methods (like vasectomies) and, of course, abstinence all carry no risk of abortion. If a baby is conceived while using one of these methods, no hormonal threat stands to deter the embryo from successful implantation in the mother's womb. But hormonal contraceptives, like the Pill, NuvaRing, patch, IUD, etc., are different. Because they alter a woman's body chemistry and physiology, hormonal contraceptives pose a risk to the survival of newly-conceived embryos by making the uterine environment hostile to implantation.[2]

In conclusion, let us state again the importance of each couple doing due diligence to research, pray, get counseling, and make your decision after giving ample time to weigh all the options. We want to be clear that we do not endorse any abortion-inducing methods of birth control. Grace to you as you both make these important choices in the future.

Notes

1   "Does the Bible permit birth control?" by Matt Perman. January 23, 2006. ©2015 Desiring God Foundation. http://www.desiringgod.org/articles/does-the-bible-permit-birth-control. Used by permission.

2   "Did you know that some birth control methods can cause abortion?" by Lauren Enriquez, November 26, 2014. http://www.texasrighttolife.com/a/1378/Did-you-know-that-some-birth-control-methods-can-cause-abortion#, accessed November 2, 2015.

APPENDIX B

Couples Connecting

Use the topics below, and corresponding questions, to engage in meaningful conversation. (Wait until after you are married to discuss sexual questions.)

Communication and Life Vision
- Do you feel you are doing what God created you to do?
- Tell me about your hopes and dreams for yourself.
- Tell me about your hopes and dreams for us as a couple.
- How could I better listen to and understand your heart?

Conflict Resolution
- Do you feel I respect you when we disagree?
- Do you feel I seek to understand the problem from your perspective?
- Do I ask your forgiveness often enough and soon enough?
- Do you feel I get angry whenever things don't go my way?

Decision-making
- Do you feel we pray together enough before making big decisions?
- Do you feel I allow you to brainstorm your ideas, and do I value your opinions?
- How can we grow in wisdom in decision-making?

Emotional Wholeness
- Do you feel like you don't measure up or are inadequate in any area of your life?

- Have you struggled with low self-esteem and feelings of insignificance?
- Are there areas of your life where you feel like a failure?
- Do you find it difficult to trust authority figures in your life?
- Have you struggled with anger toward God or the Church?

Friendship and Affection

- Am I your best friend? Why or why not?
- Tell me about your best friend, or next best friend.
- How could our personalities better blend together?
- What terms of endearment do you like me to call you the most?
- Do we hug, smile, and laugh together enough?

Love and Commitment

- How can we grow in God's unconditional love for each other?
- Do you feel you have the freedom to be your true self? Why or why not?
- Are you afraid to be totally honest? Why or why not?

Money and Possessions

- Are you content with what we have and earn?
- If money were no object, where would you live and what would you do?
- Do you feel we are in agreement about our budget and financial priorities?

Parenting Values

- Do you believe we are in unity in our parenting style and goals? Why or why not?

Recreational Companionship

- What are your favorite things to do?
- What best helps you to relax and unwind?
- What activities do you enjoy that we do together, or that we can learn to do together?

Romance

- Do I tell you, "I love you" enough?
- How can our relationship be more romantic?
- What romantic gestures are most important to you? (e.g., cards, physical affection, doing favorite activities together, date nights, surprises, gifts, flowers . . .)

Sexual Intimacy

- Do you look forward to being sexually intimate with me? Why or why not?
- Do you feel I desire you?
- Do you feel I am sensitive to your sexual needs?

Spiritual Identity and Unity

- How do you hear God's voice?
- What has God been saying to you lately?
- What is on your prayer list?
- What are the main priorities in this season of your life?
- Where are you most vulnerable to the enemy's attack?
- How can I pray for you?

Time Management

- Do you feel your life is too busy or stressful?
- Do you feel we have enough quality time together?

We have observed that married couples, who seemed to have unending conversations while dating, oftentimes reach a place where they must be intentional in choosing to communicate. Life has transitioned, schedules are busy, and we just don't talk like we used to. This is normal but must not be left unattended. Husbands and wives need to keep the lines open, from everyday surface topics to the deeply felt matters of the heart. Revisit the topics and questions above after your marriage, as you continue to deepen your connection with each other.

APPENDIX C

Household Budget

Budget Category	Monthly	Other than Monthly	TOTAL
Housing:			
Mortgage/Rent			
Insurance			
Property Taxes			
Electricity			
Gas			
Water			
Sanitation			
Internet			
Landline Phone			
Repairs/Maintenance			
Lawn Service			
Other			
Food:			
Groceries			
Health Supplements			
Household Supplies			
Clothing:			

Budget Category	Monthly	Other than Monthly	TOTAL
Transportation:			
Insurance			
Fuel			
Repairs/Maintenance			
Parking			
Other			
Entertainment & Recreation:			
Eating Out			
Movies			
Vacations			
Gym Membership			
Magazines			
Other			
Medical Expenses:			
Doctor			
Dentist			
Insurance			
Medication			
Other			
Gift Giving:			
Christmas			
Birthdays			
Anniversaries			
Other			

Budget Category	Monthly	Other than Monthly	TOTAL
Children:			
School Tuition			
School Lunches			
Allowances			
Lessons/Activities			
Other			
Miscellaneous:			
Life Insurance			
Animal Care			
Hair Salon			
Cell Phones			
Husband misc.			
Wife misc.			
Other			

APPENDIX D

Intercultural Marriage

When you marry your future spouse, you marry his or her culture too. This is both the challenge and opportunity of cross-cultural marriage. Just as the kingdom of God is enriched by the diverse background and experiences of the people who worship Jesus, **diversity enhances marriage**. Though from a different culture, your Christian spouse and you are joint heirs with Christ (Romans 8:17). This shared identity, enabled by honest communication, transforms your differences from liabilities to assets by leveraging cultural strengths. Your marital diversity covers one another's weaknesses, broadens your ideas, models healthy conflict resolution, and extends your reach for ministry.

DISCUSS TOGETHER

1. Where will you live after marriage?
2. If you are from different countries of origin, have you visited one another's countries?
3. Are both sets of parents at peace with your decision to marry cross-culturally?
4. What are some role differences that you've already noticed, and how have you adjusted?
5. As two cultures merge in a marriage union, what steps have you taken to be sure you don't dictate your cultural norms to your spouse?
6. Do you feel that your future marriage partner has done a good job of becoming acquainted with your culture?

DISCUSS TOGETHER CONTINUED

7. In your discussions about children, have you decided where you want them to be raised? Will they be bilingual?

8. If you are relocating from your country of origin, what are some of the losses that will need to be faced? (Leaving family, friends, living standards, etc.)

9. Even though you have a shared identity in Christ, are there any differences in core values that might present a challenge? (Varying opinions on work, leisure, communication, money, sex, etc.)

10. Is there anything that you still have difficulty understanding about your future spouse, due to the cultural difference? Have you made progress toward resolving it?

APPENDIX E

Wedding Night and Honeymoon

In the midst of organizing your wedding day, remember to include a plan for the wedding night and honeymoon to follow. We know of some couples who did an abbreviated weekend honeymoon and then took an extended trip a month or so afterward. They gave themselves time to recuperate after the big day, and in one way they extended the celebration. Options abound, so do what works best for you.

It may be a good idea to discuss bedroom expectations for the wedding night. Be careful to not expect perfection, whatever that might be. Who knows — you may even be so exhausted that first night that you'll be asleep before you know it! Without a doubt, you will find that as you relax on your honeymoon for a few days that you will enjoy each other more and more, sexually. Our advice is to not idolize that first night together. Dale and Susan Mathis in *Countdown for Couples* give us good advice: "Remember that you'll have your entire married life to grow together sexually."[1]

I (*Mike*) recall from our own experience the beautiful honeymoon we enjoyed, pretty much in our hometown. It would be similar to what is called a "stay-cation." We drove to one of our favorite little towns nearby where we lived, and that was ideal for us. As a matter of fact, our first night together contained a bit of a challenge. I booked the hotel online and thought the pictures looked pretty sweet. Honestly, I WOULD redo this part and spend more money for an upgrade on the hotel, but it did not rob us of the joy of our first few nights together. After we consummated our marriage on that first night, we talked, ate snacks, and watched the eleven o'clock news together. It's called "normal life," and it's what married couples do.

The honeymoon is an experience that you don't want to be stress-producing because of spending over budget. Resist the pressure to think, "We only get to have one honeymoon, so we may as well do it up big." If you can afford it, by all means celebrate to the max, but the guiding principle should be: stay within your budget. Be mindful, also, of trying to do too much and coming back home exhausted or on the verge of being sick. The most important item on your agenda ought to be reveling in one another's company. "Enjoying your relationship is what's important. It's a big transition to go from being single to being a married couple in less than a day, so take your time and enjoy it."[2]

Notes

1   Dale and Susan Mathis, *Countdown for Couples* (Carol Stream: Tyndale House, 2012), 174.

2   Ibid., 174.

APPENDIX F

Divorce and Remarriage

Two critical questions swirl around the topic of divorce in the church:

- What are the Biblical grounds for divorce?

- If divorced, am I free to remarry?

Jesus said, "'It has been said, "Anyone who divorces his wife must give her a certificate of divorce." But I tell you that anyone who divorces his wife, except for sexual immorality, makes her the victim of adultery, and anyone who marries a divorced woman commits adultery'" (Mt. 5:31-32 NIV). Sexual immorality can also be explained as unfaithfulness, fornication, or sexual promiscuity. It also includes such actions in a homosexual or lesbian relationship. If your spouse is unfaithful, it's not a mandate that you "have to" divorce. God's first desire is always reconciliation. However, unfaithfulness does give permission for you to consider your options, one of which may be divorce.

"But if the unbeliever leaves, let it be so. The brother or the sister is not bound in such circumstances; God has called us to live in peace. How do you know, wife, whether you will save your husband? Or, how do you know, husband, whether you will save your wife?" (1 Cor. 7:15–16 NIV). The verses previous (vv. 10–14) instruct husbands and wives to stay married even though it may be difficult. But there's always hope! (Naturally, in extreme cases of abuse and mistreatment, a spouse has no choice but to separate from the marriage to seek healing and protection.)

In this second scenario, we also include believers who are not walking the Christian path. Sadly, husbands and wives who name Christ as Lord have deserted their marriage and family. In these situations the same scriptural principle applies. The conclusion is this: if your spouse deserts the marriage, you are not compelled to stay married to them.

People ask, "What about my married life before I became a believer?" There are scores of believers who were divorced in their past lives. It is my understanding that this is covered under the cleansing blood of Christ in the same way that other sins are covered. The following verses give clarity: *"Are you bound to a wife? Do not seek to be free. Are you free from a wife? Do not seek a wife. But if you do marry, you have not sinned, and if a betrothed woman marries, she has not sinned. Yet those who marry will have worldly troubles, and I would spare you that"* (1 Cor. 7:27–28 ESV). Marriage is challenging, and it's even harder when one or both partners have been divorced, whether it was before or after their salvation experience.

Many contend that even if you were divorced before you became a believer the two conditions described above (unfaithfulness and desertion) must have been the cause of the divorce. Otherwise, you will be committing adultery by remarrying. In other words, if you just left the marriage because it wasn't working out to your satisfaction, you are not free to remarry, even though it all happened in your past life before Christ. The variations on this are many, coming from respected Bible teachers. I personally encourage people to study it out and prayerfully make their decisions.

Settle It in Your Heart

Have you brought your heart before God, searched His Word, and spoken with mature leaders? A decision to remarry or, if you've never been married, to marry a divorced person, cannot be based on emotions. Having God's peace is essential. If your fiancé does not have full peace, do not try to sway their opinion; this will lead to later regrets. Steve and Mary Prokopchak, authors of *Called Together*, summarize it nicely.[1]

Why are you considering remarriage? Why this person? What is the goal, the vision of this marriage? If you are considering remarriage for the sake of convenience, for providing a parent to your children, for financial help, to take care of loneliness or just because you want to remarry, then you are treading on thin ice. These are not reasons for remarriage.

Marriage is for the mature. Only mature people can maintain a lifetime commitment. Marriage changes a person's status, not the person. Are you overlooking something in your fiancé's life that you think will change when you marry? Are you compromising on your personal standards in any way by considering this person? If the answer to either of these questions is "yes" then you are involved in immature thinking and are not facing reality.

If your answer is "no", then move on these questions: Why is God calling us together? What is His goal or vision for us? What is it in this vision that we can only fulfill by becoming married? You must discover His answer to these questions.

DISCUSS TOGETHER

1. If you are divorced, was it based on Biblical grounds?
2. Discuss how you have God's peace and confirmation in your new relationship.
3. Are you aware of the mistakes that you made in your previous marriage?
4. What have you done to work on these areas?
5. Do you or your fiancé still have interaction with former partners?
6. In retrospect, why do you think you chose to marry your former spouse? Can you identify any wrong thinking patterns that went into that decision, and are you free from them now?
7. Have you received God's forgiveness for whatever part you played in your divorce? Have you forgiven your former spouse?
8. Is there anyone in your trusted circle of friends who is questioning your decision to remarry or to marry a divorced person?

Notes
1   Steve and Mary Prokopchak, *Called Together* (Camp Hill, PA: Christian Publications, 2003), 149.

APPENDIX G

Recommended Reading

General Marriage Topics

Capture Her Heart
Capture His Heart
by Lysa TerKeurst
These books contain short chapters and very practical tips on how to understand and bless your spouse. Sections are arranged like a devotional.

Covenant Marriage: Staying Together for Life
by Fred Lowery
This is an excellent and thorough teaching on the difference between covenant and contract.

For Men Only
For Women Only
by Shaunti and Jeff Feldhahn
These books contain eye-opening truths that will radically improve your relationship with the woman or man you love. They are well documented with scientific research on gender differences.

His Brain, Her Brain: How Divinely Designed Differences Can Strengthen Your Marriage
by Walt and Barb Larimore

His Needs, Her Needs: Building an Affair-Proof Marriage
by Willard F. Harley, Jr.
This classic bestseller identifies the ten most vital needs of men and women and shows husbands and wives how to satisfy those needs in their spouses. The revised and expanded edition (2011) has been updated throughout and includes new writing that highlights the special significance of intimate emotional needs in marriage.

Longing for Eden: Embracing God's Vision in Your Marriage
by Mike Rizzo with Anne Rizzo
"Hey, we know these people!!" As you may have gathered, our passion is to see husbands and wives dwell together as "married disciples." If this premarital manual resonated in your heart, I guarantee that you will like *Longing for Eden*! A small group study guide, covering all fourteen chapters, is included in the book.

Love & Respect
by Dr. Emerson Eggerichs
Unconditional respect is as powerful for him as unconditional love is for her. Men are blue and women are pink; we see through different lenses.

Love & War: Find Your Way to Something Beautiful in Your Marriage
by John and Stasi Eldredge
Couples can win "by fighting for each other, instead of against each other." The theme throughout this book is, "We live in a great love story, set in the midst of war."

Marriage on the Rock: God's Design for Your Dream Marriage
by Jimmy Evans

The Meaning of Marriage: Facing the Complexities of Commitment with the Wisdom of God
by Timothy Keller with Kathy Keller
In my opinion, this book has the best exposition of Ephesians chapter 5 and is the most exhaustive and scholarly book on marriage that I have read.

Sacred Influence: How God Uses Wives to Shape the Souls of Their Husbands
by Gary Thomas
"This book demonstrates how women can inspire, influence, and help their husbands move in positive directions. If you're sick of all the ways you've tried to bring about change in your marriage (the silent treatment, nagging, one-way discussions, or pleading) you need to read this."

Sacred Marriage: What If God Designed Marriage to Make Us Holy More Than to Make Us Happy
by Gary Thomas
"Your marriage is a spiritual discipline designed to help you know God better, trust him more fully, and love him more deeply. What if God's primary intent for your marriage isn't to make you happy, but holy?"

This Momentary Marriage: A Parable of Permanence
by John Piper
"Reflecting on over forty years of matrimony, John Piper exalts the biblical meaning of marriage over its emotion, exhorting couples to keep their covenant as a display of Christ's covenant-keeping love for the church."

You and Me Forever: Marriage in Light of Eternity
by Francis Chan and Lisa Chan
The emphasis of this book is about seeing everything you have, including your marriage, as something to be used for the mission of God in this world.

Finances

The Complete Financial Guide for Young Couples
by Larry Burkett
Topics covered include budgeting, debt, long-range goals, insurance, and retirement, plus a section on how to train your children in finances.

Dave Ramsey's Complete Guide to Money: The Handbook of Financial Peace University
by Dave Ramsey
This is a practical guide on how to budget, save, reduce debt, and invest. It also covers topics of insurance, mortgage options, bargain hunting, and giving.

Sexual Intimacy

Intended for Pleasure: Sex Technique and Sexual Fulfillment in Christian Marriage
by Ed Wheat and Gaye Wheat
This is a complete sex manual, with basic facts, illustrations, and frank discussion of all facets of human sexuality.

Sheet Music: Uncovering the Secrets of Sexual Intimacy in Marriage
by Kevin Leman
This book has a warm and friendly tone that will help couples overcome awkwardness in discussing sex. I would recommend waiting to read this book until AFTER you are married.

Sexual Purity (Healing from Addictions)

False Intimacy: Understanding the Struggle of Sexual Addiction
by Harry Schaumburg

Healing the Wounds of Sexual Addiction
by Dr. Mark R. Laaser

Undefiled: Redemption From Sexual Sin, Restoration For Broken Relationships
by Harry Schaumburg

Personality Profile

Wired That Way: The Comprehensive Personality Plan
by Marita Littauer and Florence Littauer
This is the book that goes along with the personality profile we have recommended. It is not necessary to read in order to do the profile, but I would recommend it if you desire to go deeper on this subject.

Wired That Way Personality Profile: An Easy-to-Use Questionnaire for Helping People Discover Their God-Given Personality
by Marita Littauer and Florance Littauer
We have used this personality profile for years. It consists of forty questions. It is easy to use and very helpful for understanding the differences in others.

Recovery (Healing from Abuse)

Door of Hope: Recognizing and Resolving the Pains of Your Past
by Jan Frank

The Wounded Heart: Hope for Adult Victims of Childhood Sexual Abuse
by Dan B. Allender

Spiritual Growth

God has been gracious to me over the past forty years of my Christian walk, to bring certain books across my path. I chose to share only four, with one being just for men. These have been valuable parts in God's convoy of grace and truth to my heart.

Emotionally Healthy Spirituality: It's Impossible to Be Spiritually Mature, While Remaining Emotionally Immature
by Peter Scazzero
This is the story of a successful pastor who hits a wall in his emotional life and in his marriage; a very honest and encouraging book—it is one of the best inner-healing books out there. It also gives great insight into the need for the contemplative side of life.

Fathered by God: Learning What Your Dad Could Never Teach You
by John Eldredge
This is a "must read" for men. I found it very helpful for my own life and a great resource for counseling men.

The Gifts of Imperfection: Let Go of Who You Think You're Supposed to Be and Embrace Who You Are
by Brene Brown
Brene is a shame researcher, and her insights have been greatly used by the Lord to transform my own life. I highly recommend it if you have struggled with shame.

Spiritual Slavery to Spiritual Sonship: Your Destiny Awaits You
by Jack Frost
In my opinion, this is the best book on healing the orphan heart.

INTERNATIONAL
HOUSE *of* PRAYER

· ·

24/7 LIVE WORSHIP AND PRAYER

ihopkc.org/prayerroom

· ·

Since September 19, 1999, we have continued in night-and-day prayer with worship as the foundation of our ministry to win the lost, heal the sick, and make disciples, as we labor alongside the larger Body of Christ to see the Great Commission fulfilled, and to function as forerunners who prepare the way for the return of Jesus.

By the grace of God, we are committed to combining 24/7 prayers for justice with 24/7 works of justice until the Lord returns. We believe we are better equipped to reach out to others when our lives are rooted in prayer that focuses on intimacy with God and intercession for breakthrough of the fullness of God's power and purpose for this generation.

The Best *of the* Prayer Room Live
SIX LIVE WORSHIP ALBUMS PER YEAR

· ·

Every other month we release a new volume of worship
and prayer recordings from our Global Prayer Room.

Subscribe today at **ihopkc.org/bestof**

International House of Prayer Missions Base, 3535 E. Red Bridge Road, Kansas City, MO 64137
(816) 763-0200 | info@ihopkc.org

INTERNATIONAL
HOUSE *of* PRAYER
UNIVERSITY

· ·

ENCOUNTER GOD. DO HIS WORKS. CHANGE THE WORLD.

ihopkc.org/ihopu

· ·

International House of Prayer University (IHOPU) is a full-time Bible school which exists to equip this generation in the Word and in the power of the Holy Spirit for the bold proclamation of the Lord Jesus and His return.

As part of the International House of Prayer, our Bible school is built around the centrality of the Word and 24/7 prayer with worship, equipping students in the Word and the power of the Spirit for the bold proclamation of the Lord Jesus and His kingdom. Training at IHOPU forms not only minds but also lifestyle and character, to sustain students for a life of obedience, humility, and anointed service in the kingdom. Our curriculum combines in-depth biblical training with discipleship, practical service, outreach, and works of compassion.

IHOPU is for students who long to encounter Jesus. With schools of ministry, music, media, and missions, our one- to four-year certificate and diploma programs prepare students to engage in the Great Commission and obey Jesus' commandments to love God and people.

> "What Bible School has 'prayer' on its curriculum? The most important thing a man can study is the prayer part of the Book. But where is this taught?
>
> Let us strip off the last bandage and declare that many of our presidents and teachers do not pray, shed no tears, know no travail. Can they teach what they do not know?"
>
> –Leonard Ravenhill, *Why Revival Tarries*

International House of Prayer University, 12901 S. US Highway 71, Grandview, MO 64030
(816) 763-0243 | info@ihopu.org

——— International House *of* Prayer ———

INTERNSHIPS

INTRO TO IHOPKC • FIRE IN THE NIGHT
ONE THING INTERNSHIP • SIMEON COMPANY

ihopkc.org/internships

Internships exist to see people equipped with the Word of God, ministering in the power of the Holy Spirit, engaged in intercession, and committed to outreach and service.

Our four internships are three to six months long and accommodate all seasons of life. The purpose of the internships is to further prepare individuals of all ages as intercessors, worshipers, messengers, singers, and musicians for the work of the kingdom. While each internship has a distinctive age limit, length, and schedule, they all share the same central training components: corporate prayer and worship meetings, classroom instruction, practical ministry experience, outreach, and relationship-building.

Biblical teaching in all of the internships focuses on intimacy with Jesus, ministry in the power of the Holy Spirit, the forerunner ministry, evangelizing the lost, justice, and outreach. Interns also receive practical, hands-on training in the prophetic and healing ministries.

Upon successful completion of a six-month internship or two three-month tracks, some will stay and apply to join IHOPKC staff.

Our IHOPKC Leadership Team

Our leadership team of over a hundred and fifty men and women, with diversity of experience, background, and training, our leadership team represents twenty countries and thirty denominations and oversees eighty-five departments on our missions base. With a breadth of experience in pastoral ministry, missions work, education, and the marketplace, this team's training in various disciplines includes over forty master's degrees and ten doctorates.

International House of Prayer Missions Base, 3535 E. Red Bridge Road, Kansas City, MO 64137
(816) 763-0200 | internships@ihopkc.org

MIKE BICKLE
TEACHING LIBRARY
—— *Free Teaching & Resource Library* ——

This International House of Prayer resource library, encompassing more than thirty years of Mike's teaching ministry, provides access to hundreds of resources in various formats, including streaming video, downloadable video, and audio, accompanied by study notes and transcripts, absolutely free of charge.

You will find some of Mike's most requested titles, including *The Gospel of Grace*; *The First Commandment*; *Jesus, Our Magnificent Obsession*; *Romans: Theology of Holy Passion*; *The Sermon on the Mount: The Kingdom Lifestyle*; and much more.

We encourage you to freely copy any of these teachings to share with others or use in any way: "our copyright is the right to copy." Older messages are being prepared and uploaded from Mike's teaching archives, and all new teachings are added immediately.

Visit mikebickle.org

International House of Prayer Missions Base, 3535 E. Red Bridge Road, Kansas City, MO 64137
(816) 763-0200 | info@ihopkc.org | ihopkc.org